OL' DIRTY BASTARD
1968-2004
www.klawkorp.com

GOD MADE DIRT

The Life & Times of Ol' Dirty Bastard
Member of The Wu-Tang Clan
Sex! Drugs! and Mayhem!

GOD MADE DIRT

The Life & Times of Ol' Dirty Bastard
Member of The Wu-Tang Clan
Sex! Drugs! and Mayhem!

By Spencer Sadler

Colossus Books
A Division of Amber Communications Group, Inc.
Phoenix, Arizona

GOD MADE DIRT: The Life & Times of Ol' Dirty Bastard
Member of The Wu-Tang Clan
Sex! Drugs! and Mayhem!

By Spencer Sadler

Published by:
Colossus Books
A Division of Amber Communications Group, Inc.
1334 East Chandler Boulevard, Suite 5-D67
Phoenix, AZ 85048
Amberbk@aol.com / Amberbk@amberbooks.com
WWW.AMBERBOOKS.COM

Tony Rose, Publisher / Editorial Director
Yvonne Rose, Associate Publisher
Yvonne Fleetwood, Associate Editor
The Printed Page, Interior Design / Cover Layout

Library of Congress Cataloging-in-Publication Data
Sadler, Spencer.
  God made dirt : the life & times of Ol' Dirty Bastard, member of the Wu-Tang Clan / by Spencer Sadler.
    p. cm.
  Includes bibliographical references and index.
  ISBN 978-0-9824922-2-2 (alk. paper)
1. Ol' Dirty Bastard, 1968-2004. 2. Rap musicians--United States--Biography. I. Title.

ML420.O536S23 2011
782.421649092--dc22
[B]

2011005867

Dedication

I dedicate the book to my brother Todd, who reminded me of the significance of Dirt's story because he faced his own demons and conquered them, and to his wonderful family, his wife Cathie, Marcus, and Camille.

When I was searching for a project after the completion of my first book, Todd said, "What about that ODB story?"

God Made Dirt

Acknowledgments:

I would like to thank my wife Stephanie, my sons Morgan and Malcolm, and my parents Clarence and Marion. Without them, my life would be hollow.

I would also like to thank Tony Rose and Amber Communications Group, Inc. for believing in me and the story of Ol' Dirty Bastard.

Track Listing:

1   A New Beginning with the Same Ol' Dirty, 1:15
Interlude I – The Name Game, 16

2   The Childhood That Never Was and Other Great Myths Debunked, 17:31
Interlude II – Ross's Words, 32

3   The Making of a Rap Superstar, 33:58
Interlude III – Six Days In February, 59:60

4   Excess and Lunacy, 61:65
Up Close with Dirt, 66:69
Interlude IV—F.L.L., 70:72

5   Meeting With Johnny Law, 73:84
Interlude V – ODB 101, 85:86

6   Time Out, 87-93

7   The Press Conference (Remix), 94-105
Interlude VI – Prison, 106-107

8   The Outro, 108-112
Interlude VII – RZA's Eulogy, 113-114

9   The Posthumous Mixed Tape, 115-123
The Encore – The Hidden Bonus Track, 124:125

1

A New Beginning With The Same Ol' Dirty

On May 1, 2003, Russell Tyrone Jones was released on parole for a new and sober beginning. He had a megadeal for a new album and a clothing line all about sealed. After several months in a mental ward and a couple of years in jail, his new, high-profile management team arranged for a press conference to announce the fact that Ol' Dirty Bastard was back. Well, not Ol' Dirty Bastard, but a new Ol' Dirty Bastard, Dirt McGirt.

Known as Ol' Dirty Bastard from the ultra-successful rap group, Wu-Tang Clan, Russell Jones carved out a successful solo career that spanned over ten years, but his wave of stardom crashed into New York State Prison. Recklessly, ODB had run his career and financial situation into the ground with street and prescription drugs, alcohol, erratic behavior, hangers-on, and child support, which he paid only when he had to.

ODB wound up in prison after being convicted of an altercation with the police, who said that he fired shots at them. To say the least, he had already had some issues with the law; thirteen arrests to be exact, which is the same number of children he fathered by the way. The infractions were impressive variations of dangerous, self-destructive, and irresponsible behaviors.

With humbleness and hints of hollow sincerity that surely the parole board had heard before, Jones made a plea in February of 2003 that fame and show business drove him to do the stupid, reprehensible things that he had done in his life. Though in his mid-thirties, there was a boyhood charm that the members of the parole board couldn't help but like. Scorn, pity, and contempt were tempered with ODB's likeability that accounted for so much in his life.

That boyhood charm ended up being a curse. His fans thought that his magnetism made him approachable, so when his adoring fans approached him, it ended with disappointment for them and added stress for Dirt. He grew tired of being famous at any given moment, and at times he'd be rude to his fans, unless they were offering drugs in adoration. His true fans understood. Willing to turn a blind eye to his self-destructive behaviors, those that loved him, including his fans, made excuses for his outlandish, inappropriate behavior and drug and alcohol abuse.

His charm also allowed him to take advantage of certain situations that involved women, management, and "the system". As a star, he used the double standard to the hilt and abused the judicial system with high-powered attorneys. Because he appeared to be more of a threat to himself than society, he wiggled out of some more-serious-than-others legal situations, but when he became a menace to police and as the convictions compounded, the system was ready to throw the book at him. Further evaluation, however, determined that his problems were mentally and emotionally beyond his control, but that didn't stop the legal system from throwing him in jail.

◇◇◇

ODB sat in his New York state green jumpsuit that just nearly started to pull across his belly because of the weight that he was packing on. He avoided eye contact. ODB told the five board members looking on, "When you got the stardom, you got the ladies all around, you got all kinds of foolish things messing with your head."

They chided him for not taking responsibility, but they seemed softened by his pleas. The fact that he had a lot of children to support (which they were really unsure as to the specific number) also undoubtedly played a role in analyzing the release of Russell Tyrone Jones, the father with responsibilities and not Ol' Dirty Bastard the famous rapper.

For Dirty, much money was riding on his release. Reinvented by mogul Damon Dash and his new manager, Jarred Weisfeld, ODB would have a new name, a new contract with $500,000 guaranteed up-front, a new clothing line, and a new VH1 reality show documenting his battle with sobriety.

The show, *ODB on Parole*, was set up by Jarred Weisfeld. Weisfeld conceived the idea for the show, pitched it to VH1 without ever meeting ODB, and sealed the deal without being sure that he could ever pull it off. Hooking up with Dirty's Mom, Cherry Jones, Weisfeld was able to meet Dirt to sell him on the idea. The first time ODB met Weisfeld was in prison. His longtime manager, his Mom, oversaw the process. He agreed to the project and signed the papers while incarcerated.

In 2003, everything was going right for Damon Dash and Jarred Weisfeld. Dash had proven that he had the Midas touch and Weisfeld was seen as a gifted and aggressive up-and-comer. Weisfeld's ambition gained respect among the real bread winners of the rap community, and he did all that he could to take VH1 out on a limb with him on a project that promised to be a risky venture.

Everything was also going right for rap. Harder-edged Gansta Rap was back and one of the biggest albums of the year was released in early February—50 Cent's *Get Rich or Die Tryin'*. That album sold over 6.5 million units and reminded record Execs that major labels can still cash in on white kids in the 'burbs.

Everything seemed in place for an ODB comeback. The thirst for original, over-the-top rap was quenched with Lil' Jon's loud, freaky, personality-driven rap. Hollering and raucous partying dominated the charts over 2002 and 2003 with the *Kings of Crunk* release. Nobody hollered and partied harder than Dirt, so the waters were perfect for the outrageousness of ODB and his hardcore trimmings and cultivated street credibility.

◇◇◇

ODB had a new moniker, Dirt McGirt, a new contract breathing new life into his rap recording career, and as he told the parole board, a new attitude and lease on life.

Damon Dash, Roc-A-Fella's $30 million man, signed Jones, aka Ol' Dirty Bastard, aka Dirt Dog, aka Big Baby Jesus, aka a host of other outrageous names, to a $500,000 dollar deal onto his label. Dirt was a sought-after addition to the stable. To launch the unveiling of the new project featuring songs that Dirt wrote while behind bars and a new clothing line, Dash assembled the media, along with Mariah Carey and Dirt's Mom, at Manhattan's Rihga Royal Hotel for a hyped up press conference that made some ripples of attention.

It was Dirt's behavior, on the other hand, that made the waves. Perhaps even a tsunami of attention. What was unleashed was an onslaught of ODB at his worst. It was unclear if Dirt was blasted out of his mind or just mentally unstable. Most in the room thought it was a combination of both.

With ten solid years of history in the rap game, a laundry list of crimes and misdemeanors supposedly behind him, Rusty, as friends and family knew him, was known for his eccentric, unpredictable behavior. But nobody could have predicted this disaster a few short hours after tasting freedom for the first time in several years.

Apparent to everyone watching the press conference in the room in the basement of the hotel and reading the story in the newspapers the next morning, Russell Jones was standing at a crossroads. This was the moment that happens in everyone's life that serves as a defining moment; a moment of truth, a reflection of who you are deep inside, not some insignificant, constructed persona that was imaginatively created, but the real person, psychological baggage and all. In a more perfect world, this was the moment that Dirt, or whatever pseudonym that he chose to go by, stepped out into the public eye as a man metamorphosed by the system.

This was supposed to be the moment when he took the world by storm and gave people sitting at home the hope that they, too, could turn their lives around, but reality can be much harsher.

Dirt sat down in front of the press with a jacked-up grill and a jacket from his new clothing line. Across the back in dark brown lettering was written "DIRT 718". The way he ballooned-up in prison generated almost the same reaction that Elvis evoked when he emerged on stage in Hawaii for his legendary "Aloha" concert: A gifted entertainer at the brink of total disaster.

ODB appeared as a distorted caricature image of himself. Inactivity coupled by the altered metabolism from months without speed and alcohol multiplied with the heavy, starchy prison food, Dirt picked up noticeable weight. He had the hood of his ochre-colored velour sweat suit jacket up, which accentuated the extra weight around his jowls. Like some bizarre fun house image, his teeth sat slightly askew and he looked like Martin Lawrence's sitcom character, Jerome, fighting to over-compensate and over-enunciate through a mushy mouth.

VH1 was also there to document the affair for Weisfeld's new reality show, *ODB on Parole.* Dash had crowned Dirt with a platinum Roc-A-Fella chain and pendent, saying to the small crowd, "He couldn't come home without that." Whether or not this gesture was intended to irk The Wu-Tang Clan professionally or to personally piss off the RZA (Dirt's cousin, Robert Griggs, who handled Dirt's production to this point), Dame and Dirt seemed to be taking a swipe at his old business partners.

To Dash, Dirt was a means of widening his already wide base and stable of artists on his label along with Jay Z, Beanie Seigal, and "The Crew," but Dash said that he saw the signing of Dirt as an "evolution of an empire." His aspirations were quite lofty, but they were obviously drenched in nonsensical hyperbole. Dash said that with ODB on his label, he intended "to take over the whole world; the whole planet."

By the end of the press conference, it was quite apparent that Russell Jones was too volatile to help Dash take over the whole planet. In fact, it appeared as if Dirt shouldn't have even been back on the street.

In Dash's introduction, he inadvertently referred to ODB as "Russie," so when Russell took the mike, he gruffly said, "Dirt! M'name's Dirt Dog!" Not Dirt McGirt, which was agreed on.

What was supposed to follow was to be a brief press conference that was intended to be the standard, run-of-the-mill type of affair, but that was never ODB's style. Never. Whenever he was in public, he found it necessary to seize the moment. Even way back when he was with Wu-Tang, a group of nine guys, Dirt seized his brief moments in interviews and onstage, and he stood out as one of the stronger personalities in the entire group. He was the proverbial train wreck, ghetto-style, and people ate it up. So Dirt's performance during the press conference was so outrageous that it got him featured on tabloid TV, online magazines, the *Howard Stern Show*, and other urban stations the next morning.

What started out as a "Thank you" to Damon Dash and the fans for sticking by his side gradually degenerated into an illustration of how prison and rehabilitation facilities are utter failures in reforming and correcting attitude and behavior.

"What do you think of the police?" A male reporter, who wore a traditional buttoned-down shirt and looked to be in his early thirties asked early-on in the conference. Knowing that he was opening up Pandora's Box, it seemed like the air was immediately sucked out of the room and everyone waited for Dirt's response.

Dirt pounced on the bait. "Well, I thought about the police good guys back in the days, ya' know wha' I'm sayin?" he said, "'Til the muthafuckas started shootin' guns 'n shit, and I ain't really into guns. Ya' know wha' I mean?

"I got a hole in my truck like about this big right here," he gestured with his hands as if he was holding a large, playground ball, "and I don't play that shit," he punctuated with malice. "And, um, of course, I'm gonna sue. I don't have no choice but to sue. If I don't sue, I'll look like an ass. And, I'm not lookin' like an ass," he paused. "'Scuse my language. That's just how I talk."

He scanned the group like a preacher looking over his congregation. He took another question and seemed unaware that the group was tired of his act and had turned against him. He didn't see that maybe he was being set up to be the Paranoid Schizophrenic that he was rumored to be when he was asked questions like, "Do you feel that you and the other members of The Wu-Tang Clan have been targeted by the police or under surveillance?"

This question was asked by another older, white, male reporter, alluding to past comments that ODB made accusing the FBI of tapping his phones and trailing the Clan. Perhaps aware that the question was an attempt to mock or expose his Paranoid delusions, Russell didn't fall for that trap. Instead, he used it as an opportunity to lift up The Wu.

"I mean, I ain't really gettin' into my Clan or nuttin'," he said sucking through the huge gap from his missing trademark gold teeth. "We do too many things for the city, ya nah mean? We do a lot of donations for children and shit like that. Know what I'm sayin'? We go to the jails and speak to the prisoners. We do a lot of good things for the community. Me, I don't do nothin' personally. Tellin' you what Wu-Tang do. I'm just here. I'm the ghetto guy. I stay around the children. Nih' mean? What I can teach them. Whatever. Whatever. Whatever keep them calm. Won't let them fight some crazy shit like that. That's what I do."

His meandering mind led back to the reporter's question, and he resisted the temptation to not address the fact that he did in fact feel that the FBI was targeting him and his brothers in The Wu. He began, "As far as this, man," he stammered, "Wu-Tang don't be fuckin' with nobody. Don't fuck with us. That goes with FBI, CIA, all ya'll mothafuckas. Don't fuck with us. We don't fuck with ya'll. Stay the fuck off our back. Mothafuckas," he blasted.

"The police maintain that you shot at them," interjected a white female reporter who looked like she was on assignment from the six o'clock news. She seemed aggravated, and it appeared like she would rather be covering an accident on the interstate or a house fire in a rundown neighborhood. "What is your response to that?" She quipped, certain that her combative tone, cynicism, and the outward disdain of her questioning would be edited down to Dirt's immediate response in a short segment.

"They was lyin'," he snapped. "Nih' mean? I don't even own no guns… um….I don't own no guns. Period, man. Nih' mean? Streets is wild. Shits is crazy n' shit. I deal with chances. I just keep it movin'. I know a lot of officers in New York City. They pull me over. See its Ol' Dirty

Bastard. Oh, keep goin', man. Get the fuck out of here. That's how it is an' shit. 'Cause I ain't no bad type of guy, to the community any muthafuckn' way. You be," he stammered, "you be in the community for a certain amount of time, people look at you, you know? I've been in Brooklyn all my life —"

"I thought you grew up in Staten Island?" a black female reporter interrupted.

"No," Dirty answered emphatically. "Not at all. Brooklyn. Brooklyn," he repeated, "Brooklyn Zoo. Nih' mean?" He went on, "People...People look at you and they know you. People who grew up with you n'shit. They know I wouldn't do no shit like that. Nah' mean? I...I probably whip a nigga's ass. If I got to, I got to. But, as far as pullin' out guns on shit like that...That's not for an entertainer to do to a cop, and that's not for a cop to do for an entertainer. There's too many things goin' on in the world for shit like that."

"When the cops pulled you over, they didn't know that it was you?" Another young black female reporter asked. She fit the prototype of an ODB fan. "They thought what? That you were just some other young black guy?"

"I don't know what the altercation was. I don't even want to talk about it for this mothafucka right here. Shit's over; it's over. Nah' mean?"

"Russell," an older woman with the appearance that she was really an elementary school librarian asked, "Is it true that you were wearing a bullet-proof vest?" She was referring to another charge from a California incident. Dirt had the dubious distinction of being the first person arrested and charged for a newly enacted law that forbade body armor.

"Hell, yeah," Dirt retorted. "Yeah. Of course."

"Are you scared that you're being followed. Are you scared on the street?" She followed up.

"Scared like a muthafucker. No'm sayin'?"

"Why so?"

"Why so?" ODB repeated and paused for a moment.

"Well, for one thing," Dash jumps in to save him. "He's been shot twice...So-" he sort of laughed off the rest of the answer.

"Ah, Hello," a short, fat guy with his hair cut straight across his forehead begins to stand and ask, "Ah, what kind of lawsuit...ah, what is the lawsuit going to be about?"

All of ODB's entourage of managers and handlers begin answering at once. Nobody can hear any one answer.

"Wait. Let me answer this my damn self," Dirt demands. "I'm scared, muthafucka, because the world's scared, it gets number one, Nih' mean? You got rappers and shit, Nih' mean? I don't know. It's something in my system, in the blood, some good shit, nih' mean? Just to be around children in the ghetto, nih' mean? Muthafuckas don't like me because of shit that..." he trailed off. "Fuck 'em," he punctuated.

"Russell," a young, female television producer cut Dirt off and tried to explain the whole point of the press conference. "You gotta make it easier on us to put this on T.V." she said almost pleadingly.

"You can put it on T.V. or not. That's how I'm talkin'," Dirt said with a hint of agitation.

"It's just very hard—"

"Huh?"

She spoke up, "It's very hard to put this on T.V. the way you're talking."

"You're a cutie pie, too, baby," Dirt cooed. Dame and others in the entourage who were close to Dirt burst out laughing. There's a moment of shock in the media, however, and only one or two people in the gallery started snickering.

"Thank you," she concedes in defeat.

"Alright, alright, okay. I'll stop cursing," he said directed more to his Mom, Dash and his lawyers than the media. "I'm sorry, man. I'm sorry.

I'm just upset, man. You know? I mean, I respeck everything n' shit. I don't know, nih' mean? I'm tired of my girls messin' with me. I'm tired of a lot of stuff. Kids don't need to be hearin' all these bad words n' stuff like that. I'm upset. I don't even want to talk about it."

One of the females spoke up to ask another question. "Did you have to go in to court this morning?"

"He has court tomorrow," one of the lawyers interject.

"Alright, look," Dirt said, "It's like this," he stopped short, almost as if he was bolted upright in bed from a deep sleep. Dirt asked, "Who got court?"

"Don't worry about it," One of the lawyers soothes.

"Long as I don't got to worry about it, its cool," Dirt says.

He went back to address the gathering in long, exaggerated pauses while he thought through choosing his words. "Look, it's like this, my names Ol' Dirty Bastard. I'm an entertainer, nih' mean? I'm loved by a lot of people, but a lot of people don't like me, but, hey, that's all part of life. I'm not here to get on nobody's bad side or nothin' like that, nih' mean? I just wanna…I like to make records. I love to make music. I take my time to make my music. Don't rush me to make my music. Do what I want to do, nih' mean? Just keep it movin', ya' know? Hey, ya' know, ya'go dancin', ya' go dancin'. Don't let this crazy stuff fool you. Dirty don't pull guns on cops n' stuff like that. Not sayin' I'm a soft-ass nigga, but I just know how to protect my body's n' life n' shit, nih' mean? My career."

His tangent incoherently continued, "Ya' know, I got all these girls runnin' around talkin' about they got my kids n' stuff like that, so I know how to protect them by stayin' out of trouble, nih' mean? And that's basically it."

"Can you identify the woman to the left of you?" One reporter asked.

"That's my beautiful Momma right here. That's why I apologized for cursin'. My Momma don't like me cursin'. She gonna' get me when we get home."

Momma Cherry just smiled for the cameras and the gatherers approvingly chuckled.

"This is all good," ODB says. "We don't want to continue this…um… this is…" Dirt is about to end the press conference. Knowing that the show couldn't end without some type of closing statement, the handlers force ODB back to the podium.

"All I want to do, ya' know, is what my Momma says to do, and that's what's gonna be done; nih' mean? 'cuz, um, nigga Please!" He paused for the laugh that this tagline used to get for years. This was isolated and became a long-standing drop used by Howard Stern's sound effects man, Fred Norris, who used Dirt's "nigga please" routinely in the morning show for years after the press conference.

Dirt geared up for one last climactic statement, "I just want all ya'll niggas to know that I don't be takin' no shots at cops cuz I don't want no grandmothas thinkin' all that crazy shit…nih'mean? That's crazy.

"I may curse. I have a bad mouth, whatever, whatever. Not that bad. Bad to ya'll. I don't know how ya'll, whatever, I don't give a fuck, but um, I'm a good person at heart. I love women, and, I mean, if you love women, you're automatically a good person because a lot of women don't like men. Our Statue of Liberty, muthafuckas, try anything…" the black female reporter started to laugh. The laughter snapped ODB back to attention and Dirt seemed to appreciate the distraction.

"I'm just playin'," he said. "But um," he flirtingly smirked to the female reporter, "all you magazines are gonna have to start payin' me n' shit. I can't keep jumpin' in magazines with this beautiful face without gettin' paid n' shit." This time he was eliciting and waiting for the reaction, and he appreciated it when it was received and the audience laughed.

"To MTV," he rambled on ready to amp it up a bit, "To the news, the girls, to the families, whatever outside, I got love for you niggas n' shit. I ain't gonna be crazy about it. Let's just get on with our lives n' shit. That's what I wanna do, and that's what I'm gonna do. Keep it movin'."

The entire conference ran for about eighteen minutes, but to Cherry, lawyers, Dash, Mariah, and the rest of the team, the conference seemed like an eternity. They all waited with baited breath to see what Rusty was going to say next. There was no way of knowing how things would turn out, but they knew one thing: this onstage insanity couldn't hurt Dirt's career. His formula of uncontrollable thoughts and actions was proven successful up until his incarceration. Insanity is what had fueled Dirt's career for years.

◇◇◇

If the sole purpose of the press conference was to get attention, it was "mission accomplished." If the purpose, instead, was to prove that Dirt was reincarnated into a more mainstream brand, the team failed miserably. Snippets of ODB's statements sounded even more bizarre out of context and in tiny sound bites on the radio and in any celebrity news show than they did as they rolled around in Dirt's mouth in real time. His isolated ramblings in the hands of television producers served up crazy on a platter for talking heads to mock and devour.

Dirt was characterized as a clichéd mess that stardom created; an artist tortured by the trappings of notoriety. It was and is an image easily sold to the public and the paradigm is that it is the negativity that is the positive to those willing and able to exploit them. Dirt raised the question of how much is genius touched with madness and it was so familiar that it went over easily and afforded a long career.

Much like the way Anna Nicole Smith's descent into madness was documented on a reality show on E! from 2002 to 2004, VH1 saw the potential for reality show gold in Dirt. Cheap production, high return. Executives at VH1 were licking their chops and threw production into gear, thinking that they had their network's equivalent to *The Osbournes* and Anna Nicole Smith's show. If Dirt could keep it together, it looked like they had a hit on their hands. In turn, the project would jumpstart the financial stability that Dirt needed for a life outside of prison.

Yes, the day of this press conference marked a critical moment in the life and career of Ol' Dirty Bastard. In his fragmented life where he tried to assimilate being a father, a rap star, a brother, and a functioning member of society, ODB succumbed, instead, to destructive temptations to quiet the demons that plagued him. He failed to keep the separate components of his life together and as he aged, they became even harder and harder to manage. Perhaps this is why his artistry began to suffer in the latter stages of his life.

What does life mean after years of not giving a fuck? Telling those around him that he was "just waitin' to die" and that his time in this world was destined to be short, there was a pervasive sense of doom and darkness that depressed his life and his very existence.

After the press conference, he spent seventeen months laying down tracks for his new album and he struggled mightily with the harsh realities of dealing with just everyday life. Because of this, he had difficulty delivering the rap goods with a mic, though there may be glimpses of some of his best work in these final seventeen months of his life.

◇◇◇

Many drug addicts speak of the drudgery of life without being stoned, feeling life without numbness. Drugs serve as a filter straining the laborious minutia that dominates everyone's life. Daily work habits, cooking, cleaning, regular daytime hours of work and regular bedtime hours for proper rest. This would be enough to kill Dirt. That is why he broke down fairly early to the temptations of drugs that turned out to be a major problem.

Was it the chicken or the egg? Did he use drugs to medicate a mental illness or did the drug use exacerbate the mental illness? Was life imitating art or art imitating life? Did Russell Jones create Ol' Dirty or did the role of Ol' Dirty dictate Russell Jones's behavior?

The riddles of Dirt's life will never be easily or definitively answered. Which came first? As a kid, he naturally slipped into drug use through partying with friends. After his release from prison and while living life as a sober adult (at least he passed each and every one of his urine tests administered by his parole officer), his drug use served a completely different purpose.

Working on the post-prison album, things weren't the same. Rhymes didn't come easily. "Feeling the beat" wasn't happening, and the pressure of a deadline was overshadowing and snuffing out any spark of creativity that he could muster. He became annoyed at feeling like a trained monkey, though that is essentially what being a performer is about. When people pay for you to be in a studio or on stage, Dirt knew it was time to perform. As an artist, Dirt didn't want to perform on command. He wanted to feel it. He wanted to organically conceive, perform, and creatively construct something out of nothing.

In the end, his live performances were heart-wrenchingly pathetic. Producers had to piece together snippets and sound bites to create whole rap songs because of the hard time that Dirt had in the studio. (Much like the album that was released while he was in prison.) With everything seeming so forced, Dirt couldn't be Dirt, the Drunken Master. He couldn't flow, so he reverted back to what he knew.

While working in the studio with Pharrell of the Neptunes, Russell Tyrone Jones collapsed and died of a drug overdose on November 13, 2004.

Russell Tyrone Jones's wild ride came to a tragic end, leaving at least seven (confirmed) children and perhaps thirteen in all. He also left behind a legacy as a rap superstar. With an unusual talent, adeptness for hyperbole, and an extraordinary charisma, Ol' Dirty Bastard leaves a dynamic life story. Everyone who came into contact with him has their very own ODB story to tell. With a heroic tale of lifting a car off of a little, four-year-old girl to a story of his own life that is bereft of mental anguish and debilitating fame, certain patterns emerge to flesh out the real Ol' Dirty Bastard, Ason Unique, Rusty Jones, etc., etc.

Dirt passed too soon. Fame, excess, sex, and a lot of sex. Everything that he could've ever wanted. Everything but...

What was that "but"?

It is worth evaluating what it could've taken to make ODB happy. What could've saved his life? What was the key to unlocking his chains of drug and alcohol addiction? Why did Dirt go from bad to worse throughout his career? And all the while that he was degenerating into an incoherent, drug-addled mess, people around him enabled his behavior and he continued recording and performing, even though he should have been rehabbing.

Tracing the life of Russell Tyrone Jones may be painful, but warranted. Funny, yet tragic. Uplifting regardless of how depressing. His loyal legions of fans still create social networking tributes online and post on his Facebook and Myspace pages and they still recognize his birthday every year in internet blogs. He sold millions of records, touched lives, and left a lasting mark on rap music.

He made preposterous mistakes in his life. He mishandled his career and botched many opportunities. A complex figure, ODB today seems remembered more for his music than for the outrageous figure that he was in the media. To his friends and family, "he is still just Rusty" who loved to go fishing as a kid with his father and loved riding the Cyclone at Coney Island.

To his fans, he's the beloved, but crazy and fun-loving "nigga" ranting, "Bad, bad Leroy Brown, baddest man in the whole damn town. Badder than the deep blue sea. Badder than you an' me."

Interlude I—The Name Game

The following is a sampling of Dirt's aliases.

Ason Unique
Ol' Dirty Bastard
Dirt Dog
Dirt McGirt
Big Baby Jesus
Sweet Baby Jesus
Mudbutt McMurder
Osirus
Osiris the Father
Joe Bananas
The Bebop Specialist
Peanut the Kidnapper
Prince Delight
King Bong
Rob Dog
Ol' Dirt Schultz
Ol' Dirty Chinese Restaurant
Hasaan
Ill Irving the Murderer
The BZA
Ol' Daddy Skidmarkz
The Drunken Master Syles
Ason Jones
Rain Man
Free Loadin' Rusty
The Man of All Rainbows
Ill Na Na
Dirty the Moocher
Dirk Hardpec

2

The Childhood That Never Was And Other Great Myths Debunked

Russell Tyrone Jones created a memorable character that rap fans found repulsive and lovable. If Shakespeare is correct that the entire world is a stage and we are, indeed, merely players, the majority of us are just extras filling the space while people like Ol' Dirty Bastard play lead roles. Inherently, he wanted to stand out. He was destined to standout and his mother sensed it early on when Rusty demanded to be the center of attention.

Garnering attention and being a leading figure of a nine-man rap group with limited individual time to shine is not easy, but Russell pulled it off. It took a lot of hard work, creativity, and an out-of-the-ordinary persona. Russell Tyrone Jones created one, Ason Unique. Ason Unique created one, Ol' Dirty Bastard. Ol' Dirty Bastard created one, and another one, and another one, and so on. ODB created more rap personas than what would be considered normal for even show biz. But the one personal that people loved was Ol' Dirty Bastard. Ol' Dirty Bastard worked on a grand scale because he offered people comic relief, which is vital in our society. When the ODB act was working, he touched psychological nerves that only he could touch. He could connect with his audience like the greatest performers throughout the ages. ODB drew an audience that went beyond color, beyond racial divides, beyond socioeconomic boundaries, and beyond gender.

When Ol' Dirty Bastard took off and was clicking on all cylinders, he crossed over with mainstream collaborations and became a major player in the rap world, but assuming the role of Ol' Dirty Bastard didn't come without a price.

Unfortunately, Dirty lost himself in a role that was impossible to sustain. Burning too brightly and too quickly, the energy to play ODB demanded a dramatic flash. Russell Tyrone Jones created an illusion that was laden with inconsistencies and discrepancies between the facts of reality and fictional elements that he perpetrated to complete the role. In many ways, Russell Tyrone Jones was a complete phony who adhered to the rules of stereotypes for monetary gain. In other words, he sold out. To save ODB and keep him alive and well, Russell Tyrone Jones had to do a lot of things in which he wasn't proud of.

Dirt said one thing and did another. When he created a story, the media, record labels, publicists and handlers, and even his family went along with it, carrying on the fabrication. It was all about image and Dirt had an uncanny ability to create one hell of an image.

Ultimately, Ol' Dirty Bastard portrayed the dangerous, unpredictable, Gansta' Rapper that had an insatiable appetite for women, alcohol, and drugs. Gangsta' Rappers used money and power for debauchery. Like memorable characters that came before him, he took a stereotype and made it his own, putting his own stamp on the brand.

Not only do stereotypes of Gangsta' Rappers work for selling records, but it is still a proven winner to sell clothing lines complete with shoes, shirts, jackets, colognes, and anything else that a name could be slapped on and merchandised.

"Gansta' Rapper," which is a generic tag that one could apply to most of the top names in rap, is nothing but caricature. Gansta' Rapper is a role that, just when you think it played out, the cliché emerges stronger than ever in the rap world. From the early days of rap to today and beyond, Gansta' Rapper changes slightly for the times, but the essential elements will always remain the same. Only the "purple pimp suits" and "phat gold chains" change. The themes stay the same. As a towering figure in rap, the very essence of the Ganster Rapper is to live life to the fullest and on your own terms and nobody outlived Dirt.

The role of the Gansta Rapper was played by many and it has a long tradition in the rap game. Both whites and blacks have taken umbrage with the figure throughout the years, but the more they squawked, the stronger the character became. The character traits of the Gansta Rapper are as alluring as they are appalling.

From the mid-eighties, releases of Schooly D in Philly, Boogie Down Productions in Brooklyn, and Ice-T in L.A., controversial issues that weighed down black communities were glorified in rap. Snubbing their noses at the establishment, they dodged the system and exploited their situation to "make paper", which, in the eyes of the rap star, got them even with "the man," gaining their own empowerment. Getting even seemed to be the artists' intention; however, "gettin' theirs" chipped away at the moral fabric of the black community and instituted damaging stereotypes.

There are essential elements to the motif. Relentless and unforgiving, Gangsta' Rappers live by the code of the street: get or be gotten. For example, consider the lyrics of more recent rappers like Nas, DMX, or even Lil' Wayne, or to go way back, consider the original gangstas in black exploitation films like *Dolemite* and *Superfly*, which mixed music with hustling. Old *Dolemite* clips were even featured in the popular "Got Your Money" video. The image of Gansta' Rappers as a heartless prick like Tupac and early Snoop. The Gansta Rapper slays women, slings rocks, parties his ass off, and gives less of a fuck than anyone else around like Biggie, Easy E, and Young Jeezy.

The original, commercially, and obscenely successful Gangsta' Rappers were found on the West Coast: N.W.A. and the huge solo acts that the group spawned like Ice Cube, Dr. Dre, and Easy E, were different because they were able to flood small, rural towns with rap records pushing a message that was directly from the ghetto. A turf war between the Bloods and the Crips in L.A. resulted in movies like *Colors* and *Boys in the Hood*. White producers and record executives cashed in on the hype, churning out no-talent copycat acts. Other movies, now better off forgotten, were also released.

The power of the soundtrack was realized and before long, there were other credible soundtrack releases in the mold of *Colors. Deep Cover* and *New Jack City* portrayed East Coast stories, but were produced and predominately made up of west coast rappers on the soundtracks.

Other West Coast rappers glorified the hardcore gangster lifestyle with simple, booming beats and dramatic heavy-ended bass, such as Ice T, who wrote the title song for the *Colors* soundtrack, Masta Ace and Too Short. The rhymes were clear and simple and they were laced with sexual nastiness, meanness, and violent callousness.

Around the same era, East Coast rappers were pumping muddied and layered beats. Still portraying the streets and the exact same social problems, acts like Public Enemy came overtly militant. Then De la Soul and a Tribe Called Quest dealt cleverly with issues. These rap groups put out complicated rhymes over complex beats and heavily-sampled loops with caked-on sounds. There was headiness to the message; some even tinged with the revival of the 5-Percenters' message and/or Afrocentrism that focused other societal issues for blacks.

Then entered The Wu-Tang Clan.

Out of this tradition of muted beats with backbeats, cool, obscure sampling, and in-your-face lyrics that demanded attention, The Wu-Tang Clan was born. The wildly successful group served up and dictated what was hot. Out of the West Coast tradition of gangster, rough-n-tumble, outrageously sexual, and "I-don't-give-a-fuck" lyricism, Ol' Dirty Bastard was born.

◇◇◇

Named because "there was no father to his style," as the liner notes say on The Wu's debut album, Ol' Dirty Bastard had perhaps the most recognizable style and persona in the nine-man band of rappers. The persona was a natural progression that blended the irreverence of Russell Jones with the toughness and unfeeling nature of the streets.

The only problem was that he really wasn't the product of the streets. By choosing this image, Dirt had to invent a back story to coincide with it. By choosing this image, the back story had to contradict the facts based in reality.

Dirt spent an entire career spinning a yarn that is still confused with reality, even this many years after his death. According to his rhymes, interviews (both in person and in magazines), online encyclopedia entries, and even reports surrounding his death, which were also found in his obituary, Russell Tyrone Jones grew up in the ghetto of Fort Greene in Brooklyn, New York.

The back story is even more elaborate. Not only was the legend of Ol' Dirty Bastard a product of the hood, he was a callous, merciless, gangsta hoping for a reason to kick your ass. And, like all real gangstas, he was involved with drugs, alcohol, and women. He was the embodiment of the "oversexed black male."

ODB concocted that story and stuck to it. Though some of his relatives lived in Fort Greene and he did, in fact, spend a lot of time with his cousins who called those projects home, Russell Tyrone Jones actually grew up in a financially stable middle-class home on Linden Street in the Bedford-Stuyvesant section of Brooklyn with two parents that had steady jobs and no need of governmental assistance.

And, even though his parents separated in 1984, they stayed ever-present in his life, calling his mother several times a day, even in adulthood. As for his parents' separation, Dirt found it difficult to get over it. "Dirt never accepted that," William told the *New York Times*. His parents tend to believe that some of his problems started at that point. Yet, financially, the separation had no impact on him; however, no one would know that from his rhymes.

In his debut album, *Return of the 36 Chambers,* the hard-hitting "Raw Ride" has the line, "I came outta my mother's pussy; I'm on welfare. I'm twenty-six years old. I'm still on welfare."

Living this false story was only the tip of the iceberg of Dirt's distortion of reality. The fine line between fantasy and reality was stretched to its conceivable limits later in his life, probably to the point of it being a mental psychosis.

◇◇◇

It is often said that if a lie is told so often, then it becomes the truth. In Russell's case, he had repeated his fake story of being a fake gansta' growing up in the hood with fake danger so many times that he, himself, began believing it. Russell became lost in Ol' Dirty Bastard, especially when the character became more popular as he morphed into ODB the Drunken Jester.

For fame and fortune, it was worth fabricating this fabled past. For fame and fortune, it was worth keeping his secret and repeating lies. For fame, fortune, and fun, it was worth getting fucked up on alcohol and drugs and then appearing in public. Repeating this lie and living the lifestyle of an inebriated rap star, however, was detrimental to Dirt's psyche and overall health.

If things served him well for that particular moment, Dirt was all for it. This was nothing new, though. When Russell was in his teens, his parents insisted that he always had a summer job. As a result, he worked many odd jobs as a youth.

One job that he had was selling newspapers with his older brother Mark at the Verranzo-Narrows Bridge. His cousins, Robert and Gary, also worked with him at the newsstand that summer. The boys were paid a commission on the number of papers that they sold, so for each paper sold, they were paid a set amount.

While selling papers and unhappy with his take-home pay, Dirt got the idea to separate the news section of the paper from the comics section. When customers complained, his brother turned on him. "Why are you doing that, Rus?" Mark asked.

"I'm trying to get paid, nigga," Dirt replied.

"But, you're only selling half a paper. How're you getting' over by sellin' half a paper? We get paid by the total number of papers sold."

"But, they can't count a half a paper," was Dirt's answer. Mark could deduce what was happening with the proceeds from the other half.

"Oh, shit, nigga, just sell the people the paper. You'll get paid. I'm tired of covering complaints for that dumb shit."

But Rusty was not afraid to sell half the newspaper as a crafty teen, and it was a prelude to how he, as ODB, was not afraid to phony up a story as an adult. If it meant immediate satisfaction or more money, it was all good.

◇◇◇

When it came to making and spending money, Dirt's moral compass was a bit skewed. Again, like every good gansta', he lived in the moment, capitalizing on every monetary opportunity and not saving a dime. His lifestyle perpetrated the message that blacks, overall, were irresponsible and they impulsively over-did everything because they never had anything and were unwise in the way of personal finances.

What ODB seemed unconcerned about, however, was the social damage that this was doing. Burdened with the stereotype of being lazy and on welfare, blacks can also find humor in the exaggeration of those who can get over on the system. Always playing the jester, he knew how to exploit stereotypes for humorous effect if living the stereotype conflicted with his Five Percenter philosophies and spurred his inner-dialogue it didn't show in his behavior.

He either didn't care or never could learn how to manage his money. He couldn't learn vicariously either. One would think that he could learn from one of his idols, Rick James, just how far from grace a black entertainer could fall. One would think that he would've learned from the story of MC Hammer, which he watched unfold.

Another prime example of Dirt doing anything to promote his career that would in turn get attention and make money was the notorious MTV stunt that put him on White America's radar.

With cameras in tow and a welfare card in his pocket, ODB, the legitimate rap star, rode a limo to the welfare office to collect his government check as promotion for his upcoming solo album. It was disgraceful, like a lot of things that Dirt said or did. He even felt regret and he felt manipulated by MTV afterwards.

Biographer Jaime Lowe in *Digging for Dirt* wrote that he even called his Electra A&R Representative, Dante Ross, afterwards. Ross was quoted as saying, "Dirty called and said, 'What did I do? Can we fix this? I wasn't even thinking,' but that shit probably got him the duet with Mariah in the end. If he wasn't already well known, *everyone* knew about him after that."

Characteristic of the way he lived his life, Dirt acted first and asked questions later. Compulsively impulsive, Dirt engaged in dangerous and destructive behaviors for the sheer enjoyment of it. He'd shoplift for the thrill. Pick a fight to enliven a night out. And screw any woman who let him. No thoughts about consequences seemed to enter into his decision-making process.

Several of his arrests came from the result of his impulsive nature. Others, however, were calculated, though deviant nonetheless. Missing court dates, violating parole, and not paying child support all led to legal trouble that compounded over the course of his rise to stardom.

Because he was constantly rewarded by the outrageous, irreverent stunts like the MTV welfare fiasco, the press conference that was to come about ten years later, and the many other negative episodes throughout his career, he never seemed to learn any lessons about the limitations placed on functional citizens. He was pure, unfiltered, Freudian Id. He sought self-satisfaction without filtering it through any screen of right vs. wrong, and this was apparent even as a young boy.

Russell was always impulsive. Sure, he became more unpredictable and erratic through his drug and alcohol use, but his friends and family tell stories that support the claim. His friends say that he used to steal 40s from the corner convenience store cooler just to see if he could get away with it. To tempt fate, he'd make multiple trips into the store and come out with 40s on each trip.

Consider the unpredictability and impulsiveness of his hip-hop style. Often defying a rhyme scheme, Dirt's free-form impulsivity was the cornerstone of his genius. When doing interviews for promotion of a record about to drop, a tour that was about to be kicked off, or a gig promoted on a local radio spot, there was no "traditional" conversation.

To sabotage interviews and entertain himself, he'd say the most outlandish things and wait for a reaction. For example, in one interview, during another MTV show catering to white teenage suburban kids and, again, with cameras rolling (this is when he'd be his most bizarre sometimes), the host was taking call-in questions.

Hijacking Shawn Colvin's moment of accepting her MTV award, Dirt stormed the stage with a drunken rant about The Wu being for the children. A caller wanted Dirt to "set the record straight on all the good that he and The Wu have done for their community. So, what have you done?" The caller asked after a long, elaborate set up.

"*Pfff!* Nuthin'," Dirt flatly responded waving away the question like it was a pesky mosquito. He laid back into the couch. The room erupted into laughter.

Perhaps Dirt's definition of being for the children was different than those who would consider some sort of philanthropy or volunteer work as being for the children, but, that wasn't Dirt's style. Instead, it has been said that he would stop the car from time to time, jump out, and hand money out to kids on the street. Dirt's high-profile lawyer, Robert Shapiro, even told biographer Jaime Lowe about a time when he was in the car with Dirt and he stopped to hand out money to some homeless guys.

◇◇◇

Dirt's mother, who he lived with while on parole, was as good of a marketer as her son was. She vehemently protected the welfare stories and never mentioned Bed-Stuy and she even added to the claim that he gave back to the community by handing out money to the children of his community. After Dirt's funeral, she told reporters how different

Dirt was backstage, behind the scenes. "He's an excellent father to his children." She touted on more than one occasion.

It is obvious that Cherry desperately wants this claim to be true. After all, she is a mother and the grandmother of his thirteen children. Although she basically ran his career, she could dictate and motivate her son to be a good father to his children.

The most damaging evidence of Dirt being an "excellent father" comes from his cousin, RZA. The disturbing story surfaced when RZA was out promoting his book. He told CNN in an interview that before his death in 2004, Dirt was doing drugs in front of his son. In fact, it was stated as though Dirt was forcing his son to watch. RZA claimed that when he got mad and wanted to leave, Dirt wouldn't let him.

Perhaps it is out-of-bounds to evaluate a figure, especially a Gangsta Rapper, on the basis of being a "good father," but, it is an issue that demands to be raised, especially since Cherry Jones had routinely raised the issue in interviews. And if RZA's story was even partly true, it should be Exhibit A as to how far gone Dirt was.

If being a good father is defined by paying child support in a timely fashion, then Dirt doesn't fit that description either. If being a good father is defined by spending quality time with his children, then Dirt didn't qualify. But if being a good father is defined by a man dropping by his baby mama's house for a quick booty call, endowing occasional hunks of money, and making excuses, then Dirt might fit this bill.

There was an inherent personality flaw beyond Dirt's control that kept him from being the father that his mother wanted him to be. Like any caring mother, she encouraged her son to make better decisions and to do the right thing. That bored him.

Take, for instance, his marriage to Icelene, the mother of three of his kids. According to Lowe, Cherry told Dirt that getting married would be the right thing to do, especially since they needed the arrangement for legal and financial issues. To make his mother happy, he showed up, signed the papers, and had a little ceremony. Then he went his own way.

◇◇◇

It was November 15, 1968 in the maternity ward at Lutheran Hospital in East New York. Cherry told Lowe for her biography, "I had all my children natural birth up until him. They gave me something for the birth, something intravenous. It knocked me out. He was a good baby, though. Didn't cry."

Coming from a large family with six other brothers and sisters, Dirt may have been lost in the shuffle. Everyone in the extended family has their own story of Russell's need for attention as a child. While watching super hero shows on channel four in the morning, he waited for his favorite show to come on at noon. At that time, he'd switch over to channel five to watch Kung Fu Theater.

As a child with an active imagination, he'd run around the house with either a cape on to play-act a super hero or he'd pretend that he was a martial arts master, simulating the movies from the low-budget, English-dubbed Kung Fu movies that he adored.

◇◇◇

In his pre-teen years, Russell was introduced to the Five-Percent Nation teachings by his cousin, who became instrumental in his life, Popa Wu. The Five-Percenters believe that they are the diminutive percentage of the enlightened who are responsible for bringing the 85% of the masses into the light from the dark exploitation of the other 10% who rule them. Because of these teachings, the MTV welfare debacle is that much more confusing and disconcerting. How much to heart did Dirt take these teachings?

Again, those close to him say that he took these teachings very seriously. His name, Ason Unique, pays homage to the Five-Percenters. Much of the philosophies and The Wu culture was fabricated from the Five-Percenters' cult-like ethics. So, when he pulled up in a limo to the welfare office, it undermined everything that the teachings stood for.

To outside onlookers, Dirt's involvement with the Five-Percenters seemed more of a fascination than an actual way to live your life. He didn't live like an "enlightened one". Instead, it seems as if being a Five-Percenter gave Dirt more characters to play when his identity became an assimilation of fragmented personalities; The Gansta Rapper; The Militant Black Man; The Enlightened One; The Jester—They were all parts.

◇◇◇

"I'm twenty six; I'm still on welfare." Art imitating life, or life imitating art? With Dirt, it didn't matter because it seemed so real.

Those in Dirt's inner circle who knew the truth about the lack of "gangsta" in his life were protective of the story and made sure that they didn't jeopardize his street credibility. That is until Russell's father, William Jones, talked to Sam McDonald from the Newport News, Virginia newspaper, *The Daily Press* in July of 2007. The paper ran a Sunday feature on Rusty's dad. It was a human-interest story on a father lamenting the death of his son. The article, though it only ran locally, blew the lid off of a long-held myth on which Dirt's career hinged.

"You know that story about him being raised in Fort Greene [Brooklyn] projects on welfare until he was a child of thirteen was a total lie," his dad explained, breaking the code of silence. "When I read it in the *Vibe* magazine a few years ago, my other son was here from the Navy. He said, 'Daddy, did you see this story?'"

William Jones said that he was furious. "I tried to get in touch with the guy who wrote the story, but all I got was a tape for two weeks. So finally, I called my wife."

When he got Cherry on the phone, he voiced his agitation and frustration. He was insulted and embarrassed. He was a proud black man who got up and went to work every day to provide for his children, so Dirt's public depiction of the home he provided cut directly to his pride. The MTV welfare stunt hurt.

"Look, I know you're upset," he remembered his then estranged wife saying to appease him. "Your son did that for publicity."

"As hard as we worked?" William argued.

Russell's father worked for the New York City Transit Authority and his Mom was a police department dispatcher. As a kid in school, Russell's short attention span made him a poor student, but he was able to still make decent grades. The teachers liked him, but he'd rather create rhymes and write raps in his notebook than take notes from class. If he were in school today, he'd probably be on Ritalin or Adderall for Attention Deficit Hyper Active Disorder (ADHD). However, because of his natural abilities and intellect, he scored above average on standardized testing.

Kids who love to be the center of attention and who get bored easily usually find themselves in trouble in school and such was the case for Rusty. It was apparent that Russell needed an alternative, so he was pushed in the direction of learning a trade. Sam McDonald reported soon after Dirt's death in the "Life" department of the Sunday edition of *The Daily Press* on December 20, 2004, "Russell was enrolled at Mable Dean Bacon Vocational High School in Manhattan after impressing school administrators with his scores." It was there that he learned auto mechanics, a job that he would later hold before becoming a rap star.

It was also about this time as a teen that Russell started hanging out with his cousins, Robert Diggs (later known as the RZA) and Gary Grice (later known as the GZA). These were highly influential times because they all shared a passion for music, rap in particular.

Rusty's parents always had music playing in the background of their place in Bed-Stuy. Like a soundtrack characterizing and marking moments in time, soul legends crooned to the lives of the Joneses, who were worn down by raising eight kids. The house buzzed with life and Cherry and William could barely keep up, but they provided some structure and love and they were fairly successful in producing productive adults for society. All but Rusty went on to live modest lives, working daily grinds.

◇◇◇

At Dirt's funeral, William left his cozy, modest home in Newport News to return to New York to lay his son to rest. He was in a state of shock and said that he was sure that the events were going to devastate him later when he was away from New York City, out from in front of the cameras, and back in his humble abode in Virginia.

William was repeatedly reported as telling stories of taking Russell and his brothers fishing in Far Rockaway in Queens. Rusty would always put them to shame, talking trash all along. He'd catch the most, the biggest, and best varieties off of the pier "and that was his passion," Rusty's dad reminisced to Shaheem Reid covering for MTV after the ceremony at Harlem Church.

"Dirty was like our brother," Reid reported Dirt's cousin, Ieasha Richardson, saying. "He was the craziest out of everybody. You didn't know what was coming next." It can be assumed what Richardson meant by the "craziest out of everybody" by her follow up story.

While growing up as kids, Rusty and his cousins ate mayonnaise sandwiches and hung out at each other's houses. One day while Rusty was standing on the roof of a house, his cousins dared him to jump off to the ground. Not willing to back down from a dare and always willing to give the audience what they wanted, Russell jumped. He pulled off the stunt, but he ended up being rushed to the hospital with two broken legs.

◇◇◇

Rusty was a regular, middle-class kid in the city. In public he created a mythological background, and those in his private life accepted that as a means to an end. In fact, they even contributed by creating some myths of their own. The ultimate goal was to help Dirt. By manufacturing narratives, they were adding to and protecting his image.

When rumors came out in 2003/2004 that Dirt was deemed mentally ill, Jarred Weisfeld, his manager at the time, hit the newspapers and magazines to stamp out the fire. "Dirty is not Schizophrenic, and he is not sedated," Weisfeld told MTV, priming Dirt's comeback. "He is in great spirits, great health, and he can't wait to get home and get on with his life." A quote that will later echo loud and clear when it was evident that something was perilously wrong with Dirt.

Another example is when news broke that Dirt had collapsed in the studio and no other details were available to explain his death, Dirt's spokesperson began spinning a story that all the newspapers and entertainment shows and magazines reported: "The rapper, whose real name was Russell Tyrone Jones, was having difficulty breathing and complained of chest pains earlier in the day." This story immediately died after the toxicology report confirmed that the cause of death was a drug overdose.

To combat the coroner's report, one of Dirt's uncles told reporters that it wasn't an overdose that killed Dirt but a strange reaction to an antidepressant that he was taking at the time. A few news outlets ran the story. Stories leaked into the media and speculation was reported and merely hoped to be fact.

The fact that Dirt's posse would cover up his drug overdose leads to perhaps the biggest lie perpetrated to the public, the lie that Dirt was staying clean in the months leading up to his death. To keep him out of jail for violating probation, it was worth it, but, the overall costs weren't.

◇◇◇

The truth is that ODB was nothing more than a marketing genius. He knew how to package and sell a brand. When East Coast had a hardcore gangsta void, ODB and The Wu were there to fill it. When rap was becoming the flashy, branded lifestyle that mandated a dress code, The Wu and ODB were there to cash in. Those that last in the rap game have an image, a hook. ODB had a great hook: the unpredictable gangsta' that hilariously snubbed his nose at the establishment. ODB took it one step further and snubbed his nose at everyday decency. This shtick ended up a plague on his life.

Saturated with vulgarity and packed with an artful free association, ODB's lyrics contained bizarre uses of words like "stinky pussy", "doo doo", "shitty underwear", "stinkin' ass" and above all "fuckin'", not just as an expletive, but the act itself. As his moniker dictates, he loved the dirty, underbelly of life. "Yeah, baby, I like it raaaaw!" No subject was taboo. Nothing was off-limits, except, of course, the truth about his past.

Interlude II—Ross's Words

Dante Ross shares the story of Dirt getting shot in Brooklyn with XXLmag.com. The incident took place before the release of his debut album. The following is a transcript of Ross's own words:

> *Prior to Dirt getting shot, he had been hospitalized, though not arrested for running into someone's house and jumping out a window. And the story went, from Dirty himself, that he was driving his car in Queens in an altered state of mind. He stopped his car because he thought that he was being followed. He ran out of his car and into someone's house.*
>
> *He ran up into the house and started being chased by their two dogs, pit bulls. So he ran up to the second floor and didn't know what to do, so he jumped out the hallway window and landed in some bushes. And he messed his collar bone up and got all beat up. He needed some stitches and ended up in the hospital.*
>
> *The cops let him go because the people didn't press charges. He got stitched up, but a couple of weeks later, he got shot. When he got shot, somehow I got a message from him saying, "Don't tell anyone where I am."*
>
> *I got another message shortly thereafter from the* New York Post *who was asking me if it was true if Ol' Dirty Bastard had been shot in Brooklyn and had been robbed for his gold chains. I would not answer their calls. So, I called Dirty and I was like, "Dirty, you told me not to tell anyone, but I got the* New York Post *calling." And he was like, "Yeah, they called up and I gave them your phone number. I played it off, so that's why they're calling you. They think you know where I'm at." And, I'm like, "You're crazy, bro. Real talk."*
>
> *So he had the* New York Post *calling me at my office and on my cell. While he was trying to avoid them, he gave them my number in a moment of sneakiness.*

3

The Making of a Rap Superstar

The flame of fame took awhile to catch for Russell Tyrone Jones's rap career, but once it did, it took off like a brush fire. It burned red hot for over a full decade. And like a bonfire that overtakes those trying to contain it, Russell Tyrone Jones was incinerated. However, like a Phoenix, Ol' Dirty Bastard emerged from the ashes to live on in myth today.

As a prepubescent, Rusty became good friends with his cousin Robert Griggs. They came from a huge extended family, but the importance of family was emphasized and instilled in most of the kids. Quality time was spent being at each other's houses. The kids would hang out on the street, watch movies together, beat-box, freestyle, write rhymes, and dream about being rap stars.

Out on Staten Island, Robert had a friend, Gary, who also loved old movies, rapping, and rhyming. Gary and Robert knew a crew of guys out on Shaolin, what they dubbed Staten Island, and Rusty ended up spending most of his time out on the island while his family lived out in Bed-Stuy.

In school Robert, Gary, and Russell would tap out beats on the lunchroom tables, beat-box, and experiment with free-styling and rhyming. GZA, then called Maxamillion or Justice, seemed to be the lyrical mastermind behind the trio's approach to lyrical word play and rap structuring.

When the boys were about fifteen years old, they wanted to enter a talent show to try to make a little splash onto the scene. Dirt's father, William, wasn't fond of the idea of performing and being a rapper because where he came from, a suburban neighborhood of Newport News, Virginia, making a living from rap was out of the realm of possibilities. So Dirt's dad wanted the boys to focus on something more tangible, like their education.

William was ecstatic that Rusty was admitted into Mable Dean Bacon Vocational High School in Manhattan to learn a usable trade. This is what Dirt's father understood: Daily grinds and everyday monotony. You work thirty years at one job and then you retire. As Henry David Thoreau said, these are the men leading lives of quiet desperation. But quiet desperation pays the bills and raises families. As much as he tried, William couldn't convince his son that this was how life really was; a good, clean, honest living.

Rusty, on the other hand, found a good, clean, honest living boring. Sure, he worked at it until something broke for The Wu, but until then, he did try to make his father happy and grind it out at a daily gig.

◇◇◇

In the summer of 1990, William and Cherry saw to it that Rusty be involved with JobCorp, and Russell was sent to Orlando, Florida. He worked at the Jaws ride at Universal Studios and he held other odd jobs. While in Florida, Russell was reintroduced to the Five-Percenters by another teen he befriended, Freedom Shabazz Allah, who was also sent to JobCorp to learn about a good, clean, honest living. The two became close friends, wrote rhymes together, and became politically aware of the social injustices facing black people.

Shabazz was from Plainfield, New Jersey and he took the teachings of the Five-Percenters more seriously than Russell. He went by the rap name of Slumlord Shabazz, but his style was borrowed and not as individualistic as Russell's, who was going by the name of Ason Unique. When they were sent up to upstate New York by JobCorp, RZA's oldest brother also made the trip. Again, they worked a multitude of random jobs, including work at Hardee's. One of Dirt's more steady gigs was when he landed work as a mechanic at a garage, tapping in to his vocational training.

The more caught up in the Five-Percenter teachings that Rusty became, though, the more his father started to turn against the fringe group. Coming home and spitting what his father believed was empty rhetoric, his father couldn't see any real change in his behavior. William noticed the good that the "cult" offered, but he also saw the rhetoric as toxic and corrosive. Though the Five-Percenters taught independence, few seemed to have serious nine-to-five jobs and this annoyed William. Work. That's what William understood.

As for his friendships with his cousin and Feedom Shabazz, William didn't interfere as long as Rusty stayed in the programs and continued working and maintaining some type of gainful employment. If his son could balance work and music as more of a hobby than a career choice, he didn't feel the need to interfere, but it was made clear how he felt, both to Rusty and his wife, Cherry.

Perhaps this is why most of what he did career-wise was endorsed, prompted, or even encouraged by his mother and made secret to his father. The more directly involved Cherry got with Dirt's career, the less that William had to know. Even as adults, when Cherry was Dirt's manager, as one could call her, there was a bond between the two that was based on "Mama knows best."

◇◇◇

Looking back over his son's successful rap career, Dirt's father said how shocking it was that his son was even able to make a living in the music business since it was apparent to everybody that he couldn't sing a lick. This fact alone tempered any encouragement that William could muster for Rusty to seek showbiz. William's era was filled with silky smooth singers and his son was far from that. Also, he knew that just about every kid in the projects could rap to some degree, so he couldn't see where Rusty was different. Somehow, he overlooked the fact that it took more than talent to make it in show business. He missed that intangible, special quality that Dirt possessed.

Away from William's watchful eye, Dirt and Robert put together an act. They called themselves the Force of the Imperial Masters. It was an old school, boom-bap act with the two boys throwing the rhyme and the beat-box back and forth to one another. As it is often said, you must first master the traditional before you can make it your own and develop your own style. That was the way of these early attempts of the Force of the Imperial Masters and their abilities to perform live. The early acts were more or less imitations of the popular rap in their youth.

Because he knew his father would never allow him to perform, Dirt persuaded his mother to take him and Robert to a showcase of unsigned acts. He got her to vow that she would not tell his dad. It wasn't until that infamous *Vibe* article over ten years later that William read that he found out that his wife had taken the boys to perform in the talent show behind his back. It is perhaps this lack of trust and kept secrets that led to the destruction of William and Cherry's relationship. If it wasn't that, it was the differing views of parenthood, personal finances, and personal freedom.

When FOIM took the stage, they muddled around spouting Five-Percenter bumper sticker lines. "The Black Man is God," Rusty's Ason said. Also, the barrage of nonsensical and uncalled for profanity was off-putting, and an organizer of the show came up onto the stage and warned the boys to tone it down. That gave them more reason to act out and abuse the freedom of self expression.

Their act was coolly received. Talent shows are for dropping talent, not knowledge, so they amateurishly made the mistake of distancing themselves from the audience before they even got started. Sure, in their later shows as an established Wu, they would mix in Five-Percenter tag lines and rhetoric, but they never opened another show in this manner.

A bit cliché, the performance didn't suck, but it didn't stand out in any way either. Yet, there were three points worth noting. First was the non-sensical cursing, and then Russell started in with some out-of-the-blue Five-Percenter preaching. Secondly, both belligerently taunted the DJ. "What-r-ya'? Stupid?" Robert yelled at the DJ for mistakenly starting a backtrack. A couple of people laughed, but it was an older crowd not into the juvenile antics. Intuitively, they used the miscued beat as a segue to their act by saying that they were going "ol' school" and beat-boxing. Third, their performance was a brief glimpse into the improvisational power of both developing entertainers.

There was some light applause after they finished, and the show rolled on to forget the pair. On the way home, the two were energized by the performance, but they were also self-critical, pinpointing what was hitting and what was missing. Cherry listened on and threw her two cents in as a parental guide and musician herself.

◇◇◇

As much as Rusty didn't like to hear his mother's musical opinions, she was quick to offer them. Playing the sax and other instruments, Cherry did know music. As did William, who, though not a musician, had a vast collection of albums with an ear for mellow crooners like Marvin Gaye, the Temptations, and many other old soul, R&B, and funk performers.

Rudy Ray Moore, Moms Mabley, Richard Pryor, and other raucous black comedians were thrown into William's collection of classic soul and R&B. Rusty marveled at the language and the performances on those old albums. He played these comedy records over and over. He absorbed everything, even some of the characterizations.

For instance, ODB often played "The Wino" from Richard Pryor's *That Nigger's Crazy*. To pay homage to Pryor, the occasional sample would be slipped in to the intro or outro. "I'm not gonna' fuck you; you can't even sing," was dropped at the beginning of "Shimmy Shimmy Ya." Also, Pryor's wino character would tell x-rated stories, drink anything that he could get his hands on, spout nasty talk to total strangers, and rudely approach women. So did Dirt.

Dirt's first exposure to The Wino was sneaking and listening to his father's records. The act can be traced to Pryor in William's records, but no one really seems to know when Dirt drank his first 40 or smoked his first blunt or tried crack for the first time. However, it appears as if those experiences went beyond these innocent, formative mid-teen years.

◇◇◇

One last point worth noting about the early attempts as a duo act is the lack of originality in the style. Bitin' rhymes and styles of the young MCs of the early nineties and copying the style of this familiar rap form served as a springboard for the style that is today associated with The Wu-Tang style. Their original style was latently being sorted out in the act that is referred to as the Force of the Imperial Masters.

◇◇◇

Ever since he was ten years old, Dirt had been made aware of the Five-Percenters by his uncle, who would later be called Popa Wu. When Rusty was around sixteen or seventeen, he began taking the teachings much more seriously. He watched the news, listened to the old heads on the streets, and took in all the knowledge that the streets had to offer.

Russell adopted the name Ason Unique and the rap duo became a trio with the addition of Gary. The new incarnation was called All In Together Now and they brought heady ideals and social concerns in to the act. Robert went by Prince Rakeem and Gary went by Justice.

Rap and the Five-Percenters was nothing new. Eric B and Rakim, Poor Righteous Teachers and others characterized the underground popularity of the movement at the time Dirt and the boys were developing their styles. Perhaps rap is where the boys got their introduction to the movement or perhaps it was through Popa Wu, whose indoctrination into the ways of the Five-Percenters was significant. Whatever the case, the teachings of Clarence X13 were pervasive throughout the black communities. Some boys took the words to heart and spoke with conviction while others used the teachings and quotes as a sideshow novelty act. Depending on the situation, ODB did both.

In fact, many early rappers and producers acknowledge the integral role that Five-Percenter philosophy played in the foundations of rap through pioneers like Kool Herc and Afrika Bambaataa, who studied and incorporated Five-Percenter teachings into their lyrics and their personas. Zulu Nation was a version of the Supreme Mathematics and Alphabets and any rap historian tips a hat to their influence on rap music.

Dirt's relationship with the Five-Percenters mirrored Russell Simmons', who wrote about his experiences with the Gods and Earth. "During the period when the gangs I hung with in the 70's gave way to 80's Hip Hop culture," Simmons penned in his autobiography, "it was the street language, style, and consciousness of the Five-Percent Nation that served as a bridge."

This style and raised level of consciousness was essential to the very core of the degradation that folks in the hood experienced as a way of life. With an "any means necessary approach," young blacks could steal back their dignity through loud, complex beats and bass lines and violently graphic lyrics.

In the late 80s into the early 90s, Zulu Nation medallions and "fly fades" haircuts started giving rap a style that could signify a philosophy and attitude. Considering the outrageous outfits of acts like Afrika Bambaataa, the bland black style of RUN DMC with Adidas sweat suits, Kangols, and fat gold chains, the simplicity of the black medallion on a string spoke volumes about where a brother's head was at.

Spike Lee's "Buggin' Out" in *Do the Right Thing* was a caricature of the very same brothers from the very same neighborhood that Dirt grew up in. "I'm just a strugglin' black man tryin' to keep his dick hard in a cruel and harsh world," was said by Buggin' Out when Mookie met him on the street, but it very well could've been Dirt's mantra. Coincidently, Dirt's early look kind of resembled Buggin' Out's weirdo high top fade. Through language and even through hair styles, the rappers influenced by Five-Percenter teachings groomed a look that promoted anti-establishment sentiment.

Quick to react to a movement tainted by the need to pigeon-hole blacks into groups because of the conditioning from the Bloods and Crips and typically associated to prison life, the Five-Percenters were plagued with the label of being a gang in the mainstream media.

Dirt didn't hang with any gangs, though he'd love for his fans to believe that he did, but the Five-Percent Nation did serve as a bridge into a school of thought and, ultimately, another identity, something that Dirt searched for and eventually changed his entire life.

During one of the more serious segments of Dirt's life was when he appeared totally committed to the Five-Percenters in his early adulthood years. It was during this period of his life that he was dating the mother of three of his children, Icelene.

Dirt was more of a fish eater, his favorites being raw clams and sushi, so giving up pork was easy. Ason Unique lived a more pious type of life. Dedicating his time and energies into getting up in the morning and working as a mechanic at a garage in Brooklyn, nights were spent hanging out, honing his craft, and partaking in the exact same white-man's-drugs that the Five-Percenters warned about.

◇◇◇

Ason Unique, a unique son, was around to be a father as a young adult. Although parenthood and daily work was monotonous and unfulfilling, he plodded along the same way that his parents had done for him. While working during the day at the garage, he focused on his rap career the rest of the time.

The rap trio of Ason, the Scientist, and the Specialist, who called themselves Force of the Imperial Masters made a single called "All In Together Now." The band evolved into that song's title, All In Together Now, which was a creative outlet while working day-to-day at a job that he found unfulfilling.

But, eventually, All In Together Now used some money from their steady jobs and some of the money they earned deejaying and doing parties and showcases to put together a demo. The song circulated on mixed tapes. Throughout Brooklyn, they started making a name for themselves.

Having more interest in the business side, and being more savvy and having more drive to promote than the others, Robert mapped out a course for the group. He served as the manager and promoter, getting the guys gigs at parties and DJ shows. Russell gave the group that all-important edginess and Gary gave the intricate lyrics that packed a message.

As kids with a demo and a pipe dream, Russell, Gary, and Robert shopped their band around. They took every opportunity to perform or spread the word about their band, and they did all they could to get someone with some pull to give their single "All In Together Now" a listen.

In an interview with "Hip Hop Core", RZA said that one of the people that took notice was Biz Markie, who was riding high on the single, "You Said He's Just A Friend" at the time.

"All In Together Now was never signed to a record label," RZA said. "I remember Biz Markie when he was famous, and I wasn't famous; and he was like, 'Yo! I heard that shit! Your song with Ason Unique and the Specialist'. I was the Scientist. So we never got signed as a group back then. We never had a serious record deal under that title."

In the meantime, while the trio was searching for a label, Robert landed a deal with Tommy Boy Records. Under the name of Prince Rakeem, he created an EP, "Ooh I Love You Rakeem" in 1991. Even though the single never really took hold, it gave him the inroads to other more lucrative ventures.

Fame was stalled in 1992, however, when RZA served a brief stint in jail. He was being held for attempted murder after shooting a man. While in jail, he read the Koran and other books on Eastern philosophy. He faced eight years, but later was found not guilty and released. In the meantime, Tommy Boy Records began getting cold feet in the deal that they were about to sign with the young rapper. By the time he reemerged from jail, he was transformed and refocused on his rap career, but ironically he was about to be dropped by the label.

In an epiphany, he imagined a troupe of cartoon-like rap superheroes.

◇◇◇

One of, RZA's fruitful endeavors was, of course, The Wu-Tang Clan, the rap corps that he envisioned while in prison. Under the advisement of Robert, All In Together Now began recruiting other rappers to assemble a team of powerful personalities. Robert began seeing the potential in the group as more and more players joined ranks. Method Man, U God, the RZA, the GZA, Ol Dirty Bastard, Raekwon, Ghostface Killa, and Inspectah Deck made up the original cast, though U God's involvement in the debut album, *Enter The Wu-Tang: The 36 Chambers* was limited after his arrest for narcotics possession.

RZA told the MCs to meet him at the studio with $100 and their best verse. RZA was motivated by Tommy Boy's rejection and in an early move that turned to be a stroke of genius, he incorporated his brand, Wu-Tang Productions, very early in the process. He signed the crew to his company before ever entering the studio for the first time. When the group emerged from their first session, "Protect Ya Neck" was on wax.

Their first single, "Protect Ya Neck" created a wonderful underground buzz that Tommy Boy apparently wasn't feeling because their Execs ended up passing on The Wu-Tang Clan. Apparently, they lost faith in Robert since the Prince Rakeem project produced minimal results and his early behavior and attitude lowered his stock. Instead, in 1992, Tommy Boy put their efforts into House of Pain, who produced much quicker results.

HOP's single, "Jump Around" went multi-platinum and reached #3 on the charts in America, while hitting the #6 spot in Ireland and #8 in the UK. It appeared that Tommy Boy had made the right choice, initially. However, after looking at the overall impact of The Wu on rap today versus the significance of House of Pain today, picking House of Pain over The Wu seems short-sighted. "Protect Ya Neck" appeared risky for a number of reasons. One reason was even more scary than most—there were sample clearance issues. Strike three.

◇◇◇

In 1993, Robert landed a contract for The Wu after being rejected by Tommy Boy and the other bigs. Steve Rifkind, founder of the label, told the story of how he signed The Wu in an interview with *Hip Hop Chronicle*.

> *When I first met them, RZA, I'd been trying to track him down forever. He didn't have an answering machine; he didn't have anything. And then he just showed up on my 31st birthday. At the*

end of the day, he just came outta' nowhere. I'm with E Swift from the Alkoholics [producer for the label]; we hear the record, and he says, 'I'll be back in an hour.'

"So he brings—my office was like from here…[maps out a tiny office, little more than a cubicle]—So, it's me E Swift and the whole Clan comes in, and they start performing to the record 'Protect Ya Neck'. Then the doors close. And I don't know if they set me up, or if it was a real intern, but some muthafucka comes running through the door and yells, 'That's…that…shit!' and I look at him, and to this day, I've never seen this guy again…it was a done deal by then. They were signed a week later."

Rifkind recognized the potential of The Wu-Tang's live performance and that is probably why RZA made up his mind that the group would perform the single for the record exec, regardless of the circumstances.

An offshoot of RCA, Rifkind's Loud record label was on the rise. Rifkind kind of looks like a closely cropped Woody Harrelson with the same jaw and hair line and the same nose and deviated septum. In his standard T-shirt and jeans, he looks like a welterweight fighter. Though the first, The Wu wasn't the only band that hit it big under Rifkind's tutelage. Three 6 Mafia, Mobb Deep, Akon, and many others were set on the rise by Rifkind.

But for Rifkind, realistically, a rap act wasn't a huge risk because rap records were a proven seller in the early '90s. Rap artists, though, found it difficult to make money on their own albums because the deals were typically structured in favor of the labels. Minimizing their risks, rap acts were paid royalties without any front end payment.

Therefore, rap acts did and still do rely heavily on merchandizing and live performances to make their money. That is the phenomenon of The Wu. They could make money where others simply couldn't. While most acts were selling T-shirts, hats and maybe EPs or stickers, The Wu had a whole line of merchandise to peddle. While rap acts had to band together or open for a larger act, sometimes even an R&B act, to pull off a full show, The Wu could headline and do their own thing.

Any rap fan knows that there is a fatal flaw to the genre of rap music. Since rap acts rely on recorded music and often times DJs on stage, live shows can be stilted. There is hardly room for improvisation and spontaneity, so the shows tend to be predictable. In fact, it took Run DMC in the mid-eighties to prove that rap acts can even tour live. Many rappers give a nod to the group for trailblazing a path for rappers in the live music world. They are also the first rap group to break ground on getting a rap video to air on MTV, demonstrating that the genre is marketable to the mainstream. Run DMC was also the first to be nominated and recognized by awards programs. But really, rap fans have to admit in their heart of hearts that the live rap shows kind of sucked.

Again, this was the brilliance of The Wu-Tang Clan. With a stage full of people, imitating live shows such as George Clinton and Parliament Funkadelic, there was a lot to watch onstage. A huge party onstage kept the focus off of the recorded tracks. All the live bodies pacing the stage, pumping their fists in the air, and working all angles of the crowd from the stage simultaneously, worked as an effective distraction in transitional periods as well. A busy stage took away from the distraction of the confines of a predictable show and a mere DJ, and ODB played a huge role in that.

This was by design. When Robert began recruiting rappers, it was with a stage show in mind, and he began assembling The Wu-Tang Clan as an engine that could generate a live show persona that still exists today in the form of reunion tours. He changed his name to RZA (pronounced riza) and Gary changed his to GZA (pronounced giza).

Another key component to the group was the way in which it was assembled to be a conceptual, all-star act where each member had the ability to spin off and have their own solo career with the option to return for Wu-Tang projects. RZA knew that the members had to have strong enough personalities to support their own records and their own careers, so the deal that he signed with Rifkind's RCA imprint label was unprecedented.

RZA insisted on a clause in the agreement that would allow him to shop the individuals around to other labels for their solo albums. So, every time there was a solo record on deck, RZA had the right to pen a deal with the highest bidder.

◇◇◇

RZA was a great leader and motivator for the group. He had a knack for spurring competition by rationing beats. RZA encouraged competition among the group, which threatened the unity. Nobody got a beat without deserving it. This put great demands on the MCs to remain loyal to the group while still wanting to overshadow a fellow member. It was the common goal that kept them together. They were united in the one quest to make The Wu as successful as it could be. Though they were competitive, there was a team spirit based on that one device. As far as being friends, that's not a term found in any interview to describe the relationship of the members.

Since the group was under tight budgetary constraints, they used a smaller, lesser expensive studio to record *Enter The Wu-Tang (36 Chambers)* in 1992 and 1993. Firehouse Studios in New York City fit the bill because they had a reputation of putting out solid rap LPs ever since the days of MC Lyte, Audio II, and Public Enemy, but yet the label didn't have to sink a whole lot of money into the project that up to this point was a risky venture.

It was at Yoram Vanzan's Firehouse that RZA met engineer Carlos Bess, a studio guy from then newly closed The Shack. When demands for RZA's studio and beats grew intense from the early success, he doled material out to other artists. In the process, he decimated his storehouse of beats supposedly reserved for his Clan members, so RZA and Bess then went to work replenishing beats and tracks. In the process, they ended up producing RZA's signature sound much more easily with an innovating technique.

In an interview with *Mix Magazine*, Bess described how RZA and The Wu were able to capitalize on the sound that he had to offer. Bess was able to duplicate the sounds and beats off of old records to make them sound sampled, yet they would be created from scratch. Created from scratch and being "first generation," the beats were cleaner and clearer in order to be looped for the rap recordings. The muddied beats that are primarily a Wu-Tang trademark were actually produced through this process.

◇◇◇

The 36 Chambers was released in November of 1993. At a convention in November of '93, BMG Execs were milling around when Dirt was there with the Clan to represent the new release. In the middle of the crowded convention, Dirt broke into an impromptu version of "Somewhere over the Rainbow," which was later revamped for his solo debut's cut "Goin' Down." From Dirt's bizarre performance, the label saw the potential in the group and began putting their efforts into the marketing of *Enter the Wu,* not only in America, but internationally. In its first week, it sold 600,000 units. Within five years, the album sold 13 million copies, a far cry from the group's first run of 500 copies of "Protect Your Neck" that the group scraped up enough money to pay for.

"Protect Ya Neck" did well as a single for the LP, but it was "C.R.E.A.M.," an acronym for Cash Rules Everything Around Me, that was the single that hooked even the novice rap listeners in the 'burbs. "C.R.E.A.M." made a name for The Wu in every small corner of America.

Mixing the cult of Martial Arts and the sensibilities of Eastern philosophy, inspired by the old Kung Fu movies of their childhood with hardcore, stripped-down hip-hop, The Wu's sound was authentic and raw. Simple beats and hooks contrasted with intricate rhymes and rap layers orchestrated by the nine MCs. The Wu hit the scene that echoed the familiarity of the traditional MC battles of the early rap era, but it gave fresh twists to its packaging.

With The Wu taking off, RZA put his theory of spinning off members for solo careers to the test when in 1994 Method Man's debut album was complete and ready to take to market. Def Jam threw enough cash at the act to sure up a deal to release *Trical*, Meth's solo effort (named after Meth's own name for weed). Following up on the success of the single off of *36 Chambers*, "M.E.T.H.O.D. Man", Meth's debut solo was accepted with critical praise and commercial success.

Also in 1994, RZA's loyalty to The Wu project came into question once again when he joined the Gravediggas. Complete with their own knock-off ODB, the Gravediggas released a cult classic lp, *6 Feet Deep*. The Gravediggas was born out of a friendship with Prince Paul, a mastermind producer who worked with such groups as Stetsasonic, De La Soul, Boogie Down Productions, MC Lyte, Big Daddy Kane and a host of others. RZA, with Russell, in tow would regularly visit Prince Paul's to spin records, write rhymes, and hang out.

When the concept of the Gravediggas was fleshed out, RZA was already in motion with The Wu, but that didn't stop him from pursuing his options, and some Wu members raised an eyebrow at RZA's allegiance. Today, the Gravediggas are seen as a cult classic in rap. The media tagged the group as "Horrorcore," and they were associated with cheesy groups bound for obscurity. His allegiance stayed with The Wu.

With a lot of mouths to feed and beats to distribute, some members, like U God, got frustrated waiting on their turn to shine and they publicly voiced their dissatisfaction. Some were more vocal than others, so in many cases, it was the squeakiest wheels that got the grease. Others who quietly and patiently waited their turn may have gotten slighted or put on the back-burner in the process.

Confident in his abilities to lead and deliver the goods, Dirt stayed on RZA to produce beats and look out for his career. At times, their relationship was contentious because of this fact, but other times, when their efforts paid off in a bankroll, the two were reminded of and understood why they pushed each other's buttons.

◇◇◇

After Method's debut in '94, Dirt was the next to spin off, but unlike Meth's project, Dirt didn't have any juice to siphon off of the *36 Chambers* record. ODB appeared on five of the cuts, and they were verses that did catch the attention of the rap world. He was prominent in "Shame on a Nigga," the second song on the LP. Dirt, Meth, and Raekwon appeared on the cut, but Dirt bookended the four verse song. He also ad libbed throughout while weaving in and out of the chorus.

The characteristic lines come in the fourth verse. Dirt raps:

> *I come with that ol' loco*
> *Style from my vocal*
> *Couldn't peep it with a pair of bi-focals*
> *I'm no joker! Play me as a joker*
> *Be on you like a house on fire! Smoke ya!*
> *Crews be actin' like they gangs, anyway*
> *Be like, "Warriors! Come out and playiyay!"*
> *Burn me, I get into shit, I let it out like diarrhea*
> *Got burnt once, but that was only gonorrhea*
> *Dirty, I keep shit stinks in my drawers*
> *So I can get fzza-funky for yah*

Dirt also appeared on the fourth cut, "Wu-Tang: 7th Chamber," along with its remixed "Wu-Tang: 7th Chamber—Part II," the twelfth track, the sixth track, "Da Mystery of Chesseboxin'," and, of course, the tenth cut "Protect Ya Neck" that had the classic lines, "Shame on you when you stepped through to/ The Ol Dirty Bastard straight from the Brooklyn Zoo."

After working in the studio with RZA, Dirt was given the next shot at a solo LP, though other Wu members were featured. From the intro of *Return to the 36 Chambers: The Dirty Version*, it is apparent that the listener is in for a rough ride. Throughout the 4:47 intro, Dirt slurs his speech, stutters, and botches his thoughts, a glimpse of the madness to ensue.

"For one thing," ODB says with a whacked out accent in front of a cheering crowd like he was the MC, "let me introduce myself. My name is Mr. Russell Jones…Excuse me for that one. I had to let that one low, ahhh-hahhhh…Ladies and gentleman, from all houses to all towns. From the moons of Pluto back down to Earth. Ladies and gentleman, one more time, give it up for the Old Dirty Doggy, I mean, the Ol' Dirty Bastard!"

ODB takes the imaginary stage and says, "Yes, how y'all doin' out there? I wanted y'all to know that tonight is a special night 'cause I'm happy to be living, ya' know? A nigga tried to shoot me down and shit, you know? And I don't know, man. It just feels good to be here, man. Nih' mean?"

Dirt begins ranting and fake crying and explaining why he is "here." And then it gets really weird. "I'm tired of this shit. Remember the time I told y'all when I got burnt, gonorrhea? Well, this bitch, there's a new bitch goddammit. Oh, bitch burnt me again with gonorrhea. So, I didn't get burnt one time. I got burnt actually two times. When you really look at it. Yeah, I love the girl, but I had to cut the bitch off. Yeah, the bitch died. I killed the bitch. She suffered a long pain bitchy ass go, bitch had to go. I, I knew the bitch for ten minutes of her life, but the pussy was good! Yes, the pussy was good! I just want you to know, girl, that I dedicate this song, well, this song was really written by Blowfly, and I want all y'all to hear this shit." There's the sound of paper crinkling and Dirt starts singing in his wacked out lounge singer voice:

> *The first time, ever you sucked my dick,* (aside to the applause),
> *Thank you! Thank you*
> *I felt the earth tremble under my balls*
> *Somethin' shot out of me real fast*
> *First time…*

"Nah, I was just kidding witch y'all," he says breaking character. "How y'all feelin'? Listen to the album 'cause it's BANGIN!" he says.

He was right. The album contained the hits "Brooklyn Zoo," released as the first single on January 4, 1995 and the second single was "Shimmy Shimmy Ya," released May 9, 1995. When the album dropped, it sold 81,000 copies in its first week. By June 21, 1995, it was certified Gold. As bizarre as the album was, critics raved about its originality. Dirt's style and incoherent lyrics and RZA's stripped down production that was showcased took the album to #7 on *Billboard 200*, and it was nominated for a Grammy in '96. Today, it is revered by many as a hip-hop masterpiece and one of the greatest rap records of all time.

There are classic lines from the LP that are some of Dirt's best stuff. It was organic. Au natural. From "Brooklyn Zoo": "I'm the one man army Ason, I've never been tooken out, I keep MCs lookin' out./ I drop science like girls be droppin' babies, Enough to make a nigga go cra-a-a-azy."

From "Raw Hide": "I came out my Momma pussy; I'm on welfare. 26 years old, still on welfare! So, I gotta get paid fully/ Whether its truthfully or untruthfully." From "Don't You Know": "Ooooh, ooooh, I begged, I begged/ Easy on my balls; they're fragile as eggs."

There are other memorable moments. One is when Dirt makes a noise from his throat like when he was a kid having a contest to see who can sustain the longest. This is the first, full two minutes or so of the tenth track, "Goin' Down." In "Snakes," he does his version of "Leroy Brown", and he revisited this many times over.

Supposedly, the concept of the album was to get everything in one take. RZA produced most of the album, along with Dirt, True Master, 4th Disciple, Ethan Ryman, and Big Dore. Dirt let it flow from the top of his dome, and when he looked back on the work, he considered the album his best stuff because he didn't rap "off of the paper."

◇◇◇

Because of the success of *Return to the 36 Chambers: The Dirty Version*, Dirt was contacted by Mariah Carey's people to do a harder, urban remix of her single, "Fantasy." Capitalizing on the *Dirty Version* buzz, Carey's people got Dirt while he was starting to catch on fire. "Fantasy" became Carey's ninth number one single on *Billboard Hit 100* and the Bad Boy remix featured Dirt doing a verse with P. Diddy (Puff Daddy at the time) producing the single and adding the background vocals. The collaboration zoomed Dirt's career into the stratosphere and thrust him squarely into the mainstream consciousness.

Carey got street credibility in return. "Me an' Mariah go back like babies and pacifiers," Dirt rapped. And, as she explained to *Blender* in 2005, she got a whole lot more from Dirt. Dirt represented a turning point in her life because she was at a crossroads with her career and relationship with the domineering Tommy Mottola. It was her idea to hook up with Sean "Puffy" Combs. Today, the remix eclipses the original. She said that by the end of the brief session, she loved ODB and "the way he insisted on wearing a wig in the 'Fantasy' video. He, too, was a sort of innocent. He was just so into it, and present. He loved doing what he did. Even when he was clowning, he really took it seriously."

Mariah and Dirt's collaboration did a lot for his career and for other rappers in general. After the "Fantasy" remix, Rap verses inserted into pop songs became the norm. If Pop artists wanted a harder edge and a wider audience, inserting a baseline and a Rap verse fit the bill. Today, Rap in Pop is standard fare with widespread acceptance and even a golden ticket. Artists like Katy Perry and Snoop and even Justin Beiber and Ludacris have collaborated with a myriad of others. Today, it is "smart business," said music critic Paul Grein in a summer of 2010 review when five of the top ten hits featured a verse from a rapper. But before "Fantasy," inserting Rap into an already-made hit was a risky proposition.

◇◇◇

After "Fantasy's" success, the phone started ringing for Dirt to hit the studio as a featured guest performer, lay a few tracks, and pick up a check for anywhere from $25,000 to $50,000, depending on the project. He collaborated with Busta Rhymes, the Alkoholics, Jon B, Blackstreet, Insane Clown Posse, Cam'ron and many others. He appeared on mixed-tapes and movie soundtracks.

In fact, one soundtrack collaboration is said to have happened by mistake. As the story goes, Dirt stumbled into Pras's, from *The Fugees,* studio looking for a session that he was supposed to be at. Pras explained to Dirt that he was there by mistake. When Dirt was about to leave, he noticed the music in the background and loved it. He asked to be a part of the song, which Pras explained he was doing for the *Bulworth* soundtrack. "Ghetto Superstar" was the result. The song was a hit, and the video was nominated for a Video Music Awards.

What happened at the VMAs is also part of Rap history. Pras was asked to perform the song that night, and he invited Mya, the female vocalist, Wyclef Jean, and Dirt to appear on stage. Of course, Dirt was drinking… on stage. He had a bottle in a paper bag like a wino. Pyrotechnics were planned for the song's finale, but not paying attention, Dirt was right in line to be blasted, in more ways than one. In the nick of time, Pras noticed Dirt's error and moved him out of the way before the cannon shot went off, saving Dirt from severe injury or even death.

Despite the garnered fame and the demand for him in the studio, Dirt didn't take fame too seriously. Everything came so naturally and so easily for him that, perhaps, he took it for granted. He abused his body. He abused everything that he touched. He took what he wanted, even if it meant trouble, even if it meant destruction.

◇◇◇

After The Wu was established as a Rap sensation, fame was the worst thing that could've happened to a personality like Russell Tyrone Jones. Plagued with insecurity, self-doubt, and low self-esteem, fame had a way of magnifying and intensifying those elements, not assuaging them.

Also, Dirt's shtick was very difficult to maintain. Outrageousness does not come easily. It may look like his lyrics and performances were effortlessly pulled off. It may seem that showing up drunk and acting crazy wouldn't cause any type of stress, which in the beginning may have been the case. As was seen later, it was hard for Dirt to perform and capture moments in time, lightening in a bottle, while performing.

Dirt's rap style was impossible to imitate and even he had trouble imitating it at the back end of his career. But this Drunken Master style of sloppily controlled, languid motions had a long tradition in Kung Fu movies. Dirt was fascinated by the concept of having control without being in control. Patterned after the drunken masters from the old Chinese Kung-Fu movies that he loved as a kid, Dirt's rapping style was a representation of that notion. Sloppiness on queue. Perfect timing without perceived timing. Free-falling on point.

Dropping syllables for effect. Missing beats in verse and extending and accenting unaccented syllables in words in order to end back "on the one." "The one" is that critical first bass note or drum snap that James Brown used to talk about in the structuring of funk music. Awkward rhymes, simplistic phrases and ideas were complicated by having no context. These were the basics of Dirt's style and a signature of his genius.

The same way Lewis Carroll ingeniously used the nonsensical in his masterpiece *Alice in Wonderland,* Dirt's artistry can be seen in his preposterousness.

In an on-camera interview in *The Dirty Minded Documentary*, Dirt said that he thought his masterpiece was "Don't You Know" and as an afterthought, he threw in "Operator" as another one of his best songs.

Ironically, "Don't You Know" came on the debut album, *Return of the 36 Chambers: The Dirty Version*, and "Operator" was on the last album that was released after his death. While he worked his cocaine jaw and tugged on the ears of his trapper hat, he was at least aware enough to be sure to put in a plug for his latest LP.

◇◇◇

If he was driving down the street and a girl caught his eye, he'd tell whoever was driving to slow down so that he could try to strike up conversation. With his window down, he'd pop out his head and say, "I'm Ol' Dirty Bastard. D'ju ever hear of me? Lemme get your number."

He loved his fame because this line worked. A lot.

There is a *King Of The Hill* episode where Hank Hill and two of his Texas buddies tried to figure out what the skin hound, Boomhauer's, secret was to getting all the different tail that he would get nearly every night. Finally, they trailed his every movement to unlock the key. Anticlimactically, they found that there was no great secret. Boomhauer got shut down regularly. All the time. But because of the numbers game, one would eventually give it up. The secret was that Boomhauer asked every girl out.

Dirt was just like Boomhauer.

He'd stop girls crossing the street. He'd go over to their tables at restaurants. He'd step up to them as they'd pass on the street. With his hand extended, he's say, "You're the most beautifulist, outrageously bodacious body in this city, girl. Lemme give you my number. I'm Ol' Dirty Bastard, you ever hear of me?"

It was said that Dirt got so many girls and had so much sex that his penis would get worked sore. He'd wrap gauze around it and encase it with a condom so that he could continue with his sexual escapades.

◇◇◇

His mother said in various interviews that Dirt never saw himself as famous, that he stayed true to his 'hood, used public transportation to go shopping, and never abused his fame. His mother was also documented as saying that she always told her son that women were going to be his destruction. "He was scared to death to be alone. He always had to have someone around him," she said in more than one interview.

About Dirt's outlook on his own fame, the details of his actions tell a different story. Though much of what Ms. Jones said is true, the way he flaunted his name and his stardom suggests an alternative reality. Laying a different woman every night, sometimes two at a time if at all possible, does show a person with commitment issues. It also reveals an attempt to use stardom as a mechanism to feed his sexual compulsions.

During Dirt's short stint with sobriety when VH1's cameras were rolling for *ODB on Parole,* his addictive behavior was evident in his pattern of booty chasing and womanizing. Even though it had been years since his last hit record and he was overweight and less attractive (though handsome is probably never a word used to describe him), Dirt's fame made it easy for him to get girls.

He could also be seen by VH1 arguing with his manager Weisfeld saying, "Do you know who I am? I'm ODB!"

During his feud with RZA when he was still under contract with The Wu, but trying to work under Roc-A-Fella, he'd yell things like, "I made you niggas! You wouldn't be shit without Ol' Dirty Bastard!"

He had a sense of his significance to the Rap world. He realized that the name ODB had weight, and those around him kept him reminded of that as well.

His entourage, his mother, his management team, they all boosted his ego when they knew that his insecurities surfaced. Deep down, Dirt had poor self-esteem.

Dirt's behavior suggested a classic Low Self-Esteem personality disorder. A shrink would probably treat his Paranoid Schizophrenia first and deal with his Low Self-Esteem personality disorder as part of the process. Somewhere in there, his addictions would have needed to be addressed as well.

Some people, however, preyed on this need to be wanted and would show up at Dirt's house at all hours of the night to keep the party going. If he were at home chilling by himself, one of his friends would show up knocking at the door.

More often than not, though, it would work the other way. He'd crash friends' and relatives' houses at all hours of the night because he would not want to go home and see an end to the party.

"Whatcha' up to?" He'd ask, knowing the answer. They'd also know why he was there, why he wasn't willing to go home and lay down for sleep.

"Chillin'? Well, I was over around the way seein' if ya' wanted to hang out, get a party poppin'?" He'd be pulling out 50's and 100's, dishing them out to whoever was running to the liquor store for the Moet and Cristal.

That was another big difference between ODB the rapper and ODB the Rap superstar. Back in the day, Dirt was happy partying with Old English Malt Liquor. He even rapped about in "Dirty & Stinkin'": "My mouth is sugar, sweet as a honey bee/taste like a fourty/Stinkin' like Old E/but I drink Ol' English, so I speak ol' English." In camera interviews, he'd have a 40 wrapped in a brown paper bag, wino style. It wasn't a prop. It was apparent by his eyes rolling around in his head like broken baby doll eyes while talking nonsense that the 40 wasn't a prop.

◇◇◇

Monte Smith's "He Spilled More than He Drank: A Final 40 with Ol' Dirty Bastard" is an interview that Dirt gave at the pinnacle of his career in 1996. At the time, he had already had some negative press: he was convicted of second degree assault for an attempted robbery in '93 and in 1994, he was shot in the abdomen in Bed Stuy by another rapper in a street argument. He mentioned the shooting in the intro of his debut album.

Monte Smith is a short, little, blond-haired music journalist, street poet, and Rap journalist. He's thin with his hair cut almost to the scalp. He caught up to Dirt in Raleigh to conduct a pre-concert interview with NYC emcee, Heather B for *Headz* magazine of North Carolina. Heather B was opening up for Dirt.

Smith rode with Heather B from the hotel to the venue and was sitting in the van when Heather B and her stage crew arrived after her set. While Smith was going over some notes and trying to prepare some questions for Dirt's interview, the stage crew was unusually quiet after the show, and Heather B looked agitated. As they were waiting to depart, her stage manager runs to the van screaming, "What did he do? What did he do?"

"Just leave me alone," Heather B screamed back. "I took care of it."

Scanning the faces on the van, her manager said, "I don't give a fuck who he is. Let's go get that muthafucka!"

As for how the situation turned out, Smith wrote, "I started having a bad feeling he was talking about Dirty because at that exact moment where we were receiving the pep rally, I could see Ol' Dirty and his mob of forty or more exiting the venue. Once the road manager saw their numbers, he quickly calmed down, asked if everyone was in, slid into the driver's seat and drove us back to the hotel. No one said a word. I found out later that night that Ol' Dirty had allegedly followed Heather B into the VIP bathroom at the venue and tried to get physical. When I questioned both artists about the incident the following morning, both declined to comment."

Smith's interview with Dirt took place on April 6, 1996 in a Best Western hotel bathroom. Dirt's entourage, about 40 deep, were in the main room partying, smoking blunts and drinking 40s. Smith "had the chance to sit back and listen to Ol' Dirty Bastard in prime intoxicated form," he wrote. That night, between betting me his shoes over whether or not he fucked Mariah Carey in the ass and breaking down the day's mathematics, ODB told me that he was living the best days of his life."

In the course of the interview, Smith asked, "In the parking lot tonight after the show, it looked like you had a small army with you. Who are they and are you paying the bill for all those muthafuckas to be on tour?" He laughed to sugar coat getting personal, and Dirt joined him in laughter.

"That was the Brooklyn Zoo, my brothers!" Dirt responded. "And there's enough money for all of us. I can't be around my brothers and I got money and they ain't got no money because if I got money, I gotta split it with these muthafuckas anyway. So, if we all have our own currency and our babies have their own currency and their babies' babies have their own, then you have a nation of people that have money and when you have money, you can make power moves."

Dirt took a swig of his 40 while Smith asked the next question, "Speaking of money, the Mariah Carey collaboration turned out to be a very lucrative one. Are there any other mainstream artists you're considering working with?"

"Prince and myself are getting ready to do a song together. Who else?" Dirt's mind began turning over names. "The Red Hot Chile Peppers, Lenny Kravits and I would just like to say that *they* called ME!" He laughed. "My brother has a heavy metal band called Funk Face. We're teaming up. Whatever comes to mind, I'm gonna do. I don't give a fuck! Country Western, Jazz, R&B, Rock N' Roll, Heavy Metal, fuck pussy while rhyming," he laughed again, "as long as it's got to do with money, I'm gonna do it."

After a few questions with some long-winded and semi-coherent answers, Smith asked, "You mentioned GZA was the 'foundation,' but I've read RZA is who inspired you to pursue writing and music. Who first helped in transforming Russell Jones into Ol' Dirty Bastard?"

"GZA's the foundation, RZA's the manifestation of Wu-Tang, and Ol' Dirty is just the understanding of it," Dirt explained through the haze of the beer and pot. "The reason I say GZA is the foundation is because he was the one who actually sat down with RZA and taught Rakeem, RZA, how to rhyme. Then RZA taught me knowledge of self and knowledge of Rap and if I didn't study my lessons, RZA would bust my ass, so I had no choice."

"So RZA was more of a father-figure than a friend?"

"Hell yeah! Listen…he used to write my shit down on paper for me. At the time, I didn't like to rhyme. Who the fuck wanna' read shit off paper? I didn't even like going to fucking school. Nih' mean? But he made me do it because he saw the light in me. If it wasn't for RZA, The Wu wouldn't be shit."

The interview ended when Dirt ended up spilling his beer.

Dirt was having the time of his life, but as he would soon learn, there is such a thing as too much of a good thing.

Interlude IV

Six days in February 1998 exemplify how tumultuous Dirt's life was. Though there were other hellacious weeks in his life, this might be one of the most awe-inspiring. It shows how dramatically the peaks and valleys of his life contrasted.

SATURDAY—February 21, 1998—Dirt was hanging out at Popa Wu's Brooklyn Sounds studio on Fulton Street in Bed Stuy during a Wu affiliate Twelve O'Clock recording session. While he was looking out the window, he happened to witness a 1996 Mustang lose control and run over a little four-year-old girl. In a panic, Dirt ran screaming out of the studio to rush to the girl's aid.

With band mates following, Dirt found the girl pinned under the car, so they elicited help from some onlookers who lifted the car enough for Dirt to free her. She was rushed to the Kings County Hospital and treated with first and second degree burns from the engine.

As a side note, Mariah Carey finished up her "Butterfly Tour" on this date. She did the "Fantasy Bad Boy Remix" and Dirt was there in the form of a pre-recorded audio.

SUNDAY—February 22, 1998—Dirt and his friends visited the little girl in the hospital under an alias, but the girl's sister recognized him from being a fan. She told her parents, Ben and Maxine Lovell, who the men were. In more of a gesture of gratitude than to get attention, they alerted the media.

MONDAY—February 23, 1998—Dirt stopped by MTV Radio Network to announce My Dirty Wear clothing line that was still in development. Though it never got off the ground, Dirt said that the line would feature design input from "Me, myself, and my mamma. We're going to bring in designers, whatever's clever, whatever works. My mind is open to all suggestions."

Dirt's publicists and managers became aware of the car accident only after the *New York Daily News* called for comment.

TUESDAY—February 24, 1998—*The New York Daily News* runs a detailed story of Dirt saving "little Maati Lovell" and they give the mother's eyewitness account of what happened. "…Maati hit the car and rolled on the hood…Some brothers came from out of nowhere… She didn't know what happened."

WEDNESDAY—February 25, 1998—That night, Dirt bum-rushed the stage at the Grammys—a night that will live in infamy. When asked backstage why he did it by Chris Connelly from MTV News, Dirt said, "Something just jumped into my blood."

Dirt's "performance" at the Grammys drowned out any hope of his heroism being the top story. Instead, every media outlet focused solely on how much of a spectacle Dirt was under the glitz and glamour of the Grammys. His line, "The Wu is for the children" was more mocked than praised, regardless of the events that took place on Saturday.

THURSDAY—February 26, 1998—MTV News ran a detailed story in which they try to explain Dirt's actions at the Grammys.

4

Excess And Lunacy

Russell Tyrone Jones's addictive personality hooked him on fame. Hooked him on sex. Hooked him on drugs. And, hooked him on a lifestyle that would eventually lead to destruction.

As Ol' Dirty Bastard became more famous, his devolution could be seen through appearances on television, news casts, tabloid magazines, and his music. The partying videos, the classic MTV incidents, the bizarre interviews in print and on video all came from this critical period in Dirt's life between 1997 to his being sent to rehab in 2000. Yet, these were the years that Dirt seemed to look back on with the most fondness when he felt washed up by 35 in 2003.

As the money rolled in, Dirt was able to afford more expensive drugs. When he wasn't buying drugs, fans and friends were slipping them to him. The nights were measured in clubs, women, and outbursts.

Probably the most lucrative period of his career came during this most tumultuous period of his personal life. It suggests a correlation between the trouble that a rapper gets into and that rapper's success.

◇◇◇

In early 1997, RZA had the concept of an operatic version of a Rap album, something that has yet to be attempted. He wanted to call the release *The 8th Diagram*, inspired by one of his favorite Kung Fu movies,

The Eight Diagram Pole Fighters. The Clan members weren't receptive to the idea, however. Instead, they set to work completing and polishing, releasing and promoting *Wu-Tang Forever* in early June of that year. The album sold over 600,000 copies in its first week and within a couple of months, it ended up going number one worldwide.

Wu-Tang Forever, a double CD, was a sure-fire money maker because of the anticipation for a follow-up to their debut and the solo projects that it spawned over the last few years. The Wu brand was established and the merchandising and clothing line was extremely fruitful. The sales for the release were strong and for the most part, it was critically accepted.

Some critics, on the other hand, knocked the lack of cohesion, the long, stream-of-consciousness songs, and lyrics that were Five-Percenter rhetoric. Also, critics made note of the varied production quality, which wasn't bad, but different from what was typical Wu style (RZA turned some of the duties over to protégés True Master and 4th Disciple). The fans also seemed to agree with the critics that there was an inordinate amount of "filler" on the album. Despite these elements, to date, the album has sold over 8.3 million copies worldwide, making it the best selling album in their catalog.

This album featured a new amped-up sound that now incorporated a thickness in the music that contrasted with the stripped-down sound that was associated with The Wu's style. The LP was also nominated for a Grammy for Best Rap Album, and Dirt appeared on six out of the twenty five cuts. In fact, he even had a solo on the second LP entitled "Dog Shit," a song as filthy as its name.

To promote the release, The Wu hit the road with Rage Against the Machine for a summer tour, but only a few shows were able to boast about having all nine of the members present. RZA was frustrated by having sporadic involvement by the members, and Dirt was obviously one of the greatest offenders of promising to be at a show and then missing it altogether without a legitimate excuse. Eventually, the Clan dropped out of the tour citing "internal conflicts" as the reason.

An arrest that would lead to other legal complications took place soon following. Icelene charged him for being over $35,000 behind in child support for the three children that they had together. If Dirt would've taken care of the issue properly, the problem would've probably faded away. But, either out of spite or negligence, Dirt made no effort to rectify the situation, and this problem lingered and legally snowballed for years. He missed court dates. Bench warrants were issued, and leans on Dirt's music-business affairs were levied.

◇◇◇

By the time his second solo album, *Nigga Please,* was to be released after hit-and-miss attempts in the studio, Dirt went off the deep end. It was one arrest after another. It seemed as if each night left everybody with a wild tale of debauchery, indulgence, drug use, danger, or quirkiness.

The internet is flooded with stories. Some of them read like a bizarre porno script, like the time that he was on the tour bus in Greensboro, North Carolina on The Wu Forever tour. Ghostface and Raekwon said that the crew was able to instigate a fight between two strippers who were riding with the group. One of the women attacked the other with a knife, and stabbed her in the leg. That didn't stop Dirt from wanting to play with her vagina though, because he ended up on the floor with his fingers in it while everyone else was shocked and horrified.

Some of the stories reveal Dirt's incompetence while inebriated, like one of his shows where he laid strewn across a speaker. His stage mates grew used to taking the show over for Dirt as these types of problems became a more common occurrence. At the time, though, this was fairly new to the posse. They repeated songs and stretched the show out as long as they could. The fans became agitated when they ripped into "Brooklyn Zoo" for the third time. Dirt was helped up and led offstage, and the show ended short.

Some of the stories reveal how abrasive, argumentative, or perhaps even violent he could become when he couldn't get his way, like his arrest at the House of Blues when he threatened a bouncer who ejected him for his drunken behavior.

◇◇◇

If Dirt has a magnum opus that remains an emblem from the most insane portion of his life, it would have to be *Nigga Please,* an eerie, but hauntingly irresistible showcase of Dirt's subconscious.

Because of RZA's inability to get Dirt "focused," it took a long time for them to finish the project. It was February of '99 that the duo "got serious" about the LP's completion because of the pressure exerted by Elektra. "But when it came time to assemble the album," RZA said in an interview with *Rolling Stone*, "we listened to a lot of old Blowfly and Richard Pryor tapes, just buggin' out. I told Elektra [CEO Sylvia Rhone] that ODB wants a Grammy, but fuck going for the hip-hop Grammy; this shit is funny—let's go for the comedy Grammy!"

To capitalize on the trends of the time and to mix up tones and sounds, Dirt and RZA went to other producers, like Irv Gotti (Jay Z, DMX, Ja Rule), Pharrell Williams (The Neptunes, Snoop Dogg, Britney Spears), and good friend Buddha Monk. Rhone was sensitive to the vulgarity on the record. She said, ""I have my own opinions, but I have a responsibility to the artists to let them do their art. I've got to let Dirty be Dirty."

And Dirty was dirty. Like the spontaneity of his debut, *Nigga Please* just happened to happen. Chris Rock just happened to be in the building at the same time Dirt was recording "Recognize" and he added to the track. Gotti said "I Can't Wait" was conceived, recorded, overlapped, and banged out in two to three hours.

Buddha Monk told a story about one of his sessions with Dirt: "At one session I was at, we were really off our motherfuckin' rockers—we were high as hell. I was seeing twins, I was so drunk. And we'd go to the bathroom and somebody would be in there sniffin' coke! And Dirty always has women at his sessions. We're all ready to do the song and this girl wants to get on the album. We put the track on and let her start singing. Then Dirty was in there, fucking her in her ass while the track was rolling. He was hitting her head against the drum —that's why you be hearing funny sounds on the track."

RZA explained how "Good Morning Heartbreak" came about. "Last summer, after he got shot, Dirty ran out of the hospital and I found him at his father's house. I picked him up and said, 'Hang out with me for a month.' We just drove through Ohio, through Boston; we had no destination. He still had his bandages on and he had a Natalie Cole tape in his pocket that had 'Good Morning Heartache' on it. He put it in and started singing along. There was a van full of us and tears were coming from all of us. We could feel the heartache that he goes through. He feels like he can't turn nowhere for that love that every man needs. We must've listened to that song a hundred times during our travels. I said to him, 'I need you to do this song on your album—I need people to feel how you felt going through this.' I wanted him to do it with his roommate. He didn't want to do that, so we got a studio singer [Lil' Mo] with a nice voice. It adds a nice mood to the album. It takes you out of the comedy and puts you right into the world of his pain."

Like for his debut album, Dirt was the creator of his album cover. It was his idea to put his welfare card on *The Dirty Version,* and according to Alli Truch, Vice President of Creative Service for Elektra, Dirt came up with the cover art for *Nigga Please.* "When I met with Dirty to talk about his concept for the album cover, he told me that he wanted to look like Rick James because he was doing a cover of [James'] 'Cold Blooded,' and he thought it would be funny. All he asked me for was a Rick James outfit and a Donna Summer outfit. He ended up wearing the Donna Summer wig with the Rick James outfit. As you know, Dirty is very creative."

Though the album does not suit mainstream tastes, the album was critically and commercially successful. It peaked at #2 on Billboard's Top R&B/Hip Hop chart and #10 on the Billboard's 200. But critics who missed Dirt's style slammed his singing abilities as "laughable," totally missing the point while calling his covers "miscues."

◇◇◇

Though *Nigga Please* may not suit everyone's musical tastes, no one can deny the album's honesty. The integrity. The fearlessness of an artist exposing a part of himself that most would assuredly suppress. *Nigga Please* is bittersweet.

The album represents a tortured artist laughing at himself while working through issues breached only on a therapist's couch. Though not as artful as other works, we are slapped in the face with unapproachable realism and a descent into madness.

Up Close with DIRT

Interlude IV—F.L.L.

In Chung King Recording Studio's lobby, pictures of LL Cool J and Gold and Platinum Record Plaques don the walls. Dirt sits in the middle of a black leather sectional. He is flanked by Chris Lighty of Violator Management, LL Cool J's manager. There's two other men beside Lighty. Dante Ross, Dirt's manager, and one of Dirt's friends, Crazy Sam, another rapper, who is on Dirt's other side.

LIGHTY: I want to thank you guys for coming down… and so fast! That's how LL and I like to get things done. Dirt is on fire right now and we thought it would be a good idea to get LL and Dirt on a song together.

ROSS: We're thankful for the opportunity to work with LL. He's an established name. Dirt jumped at the opportunity. We appreciate you guys thinking of us.

LIGHTY: Then we're set then. Let's get Dirt into the studio. He could just freestyle and do what he does.

ROSS: Right. Let's do this. Ready Dirt? You ready to throw down some freestyle?

Dirt is in the booth, headphones on, microphone hot.

DIRT: Cut, cut, cut, man. I ain't feelin' it, man. I ain't feelin' it.

VOICE BEHIND
THE GLASS: We've been working this track for some time now, Dirt. We've put a lot of time into this already. Are we going to be able to do this today?

Lighty enters the studio.

LIGHTY: Yo', my man, what are we doing here? You're wasting our time.

DIRT: LL?! LL wants me to rap on a song?! Fuck LL!

LIGHTY: Excuse me?

DIRT: Fuck LL!

Dirt storms out of the studio and back out into the lobby. He grabs a Platinum Record plaque from the wall and throws it on the floor.

DIRT: I'mma piss on LL.

ROSS: Yo', Dirt. What the fuck are you doin'?

DIRT: I don't even give a fuck. LL ain't shit. I don't give a shit about LL. I'mma piss on that nigga.

LIGHTY: Look, enough is enough! Get this crazy mutha-fucka outta here. Session's over. Get 'im outta here.

CRAZY SAM: Wait a minute, nigga. Who you tellin' that the fuckin' session's over? It ain't over 'til we say it's over.

DIRT: (undoing his pants) I'mma pee on LL.

Lighty and his men reach on their hips and pull their weapons while Crazy Sam pulls his. It is a Mexican Standoff in the lobby of the studio.

ROSS: Chris, Chris, Dirt's outta his mind today. Let's all calm the fuck down. He don't mean it. He's just not himself today. Let us slide, man. Come on. You know he don't mean it.

Ross slowly reaches out to Lighty. The two head for the elevators. Dirt and Crazy Sam remain in the lobby.

LIGHTY: Just get those niggas the fuck outta here, dude. And don't come back. I don't want to hear shit about Ol' Dirty Bastard.

ROSS: Word, Chris. I'm sorry, man. I'm sorry, Chris. Dirt's sorry. We didn't want things to go down like this.

Dirt enters the elevators zipping up his pants. There's a ding. The doors open, and Dirt, Crazy Sam, and Ross enter the elevator. The doors close.

5

Meeting With Johnny Law

Russell Tyrone Jones used to play a superhero crime fighter as a kid, but as an adult, he ended up living the life of a criminal.

He didn't intend it to be that way, it just happened that way. As the fame increased, the level of seriousness increased, probably because the level of drug use and paranoia increased.

To alleviate confusion for the chapter, it is easiest to start by giving a timeline of Dirt's incidents and arrests.

1993	2nd degree assault in a robbery attempt
1994	Shot in the abdomen by another rapper
1997	The child support arrest
Early 1998	Domestic abuse
May 20, 1998	Appeared in court as a deadbeat dad, owing over $35,000 in unpaid child support for his three kids to Icelene
June 30, 1998	Shot in the back during an alleged robbery at his cousin's Brooklyn apartment
July 4, 1998	Arrested for stealing a pair of sneakers from Sneaker Stadium in Virginia Beach, VA—not far

	from his father's house, who he was visiting at the time
August 13, 1998	Skipping court dates for the shoplifting arrest, fines and charges mounted when three warrants for his arrest were issued
September 5, 1998	Dirt was kicked out of a Four Seasons Hotel in Berlin, Germany for lounging nude on the balcony. No charges were filed.
September 17, 1998	Arrested for making terroristic threats to a House of Blues bouncer in West Hollywood
October 8, 1998	Skipped this court date in CA to answer the charge of three felony counts from the incident
November 6, 1998	Arrested in Carson, CA for harassing another baby mamma at her workplace and threatened her life. Bail was set at $500,000. It was posted and he walked.
January 16, 1999	Alleged shootout with Brooklyn police
February 16, 1999	Arrested for wearing a bullet proof vest, which was against a new California law
March 22, 1999	Arrested for possessing three vials of crack
May 18, 1999	For the second time this month, ODB showed up at the wrong courthouse in California. According to the LA Superior Court clerk, Dirt showed up at Santa Monica Superior Court, where Judge Richard Berry postponed the hearing.
August 2, 1999	Arrested in Queens with crack and marijuana
August 12, 1999	A warrant was released when he failed to appear in court for the arraignment hearing for his bulletproof vest violation

August 13, 1999—Sent to Impact House in Carmel, NY for court-ordered rehab

January 18, 2000	Discharged from Impact House for noncompliance and sent to jail in LA
January 19, 2000	A Queens Criminal Court judge issued a bench warrant for Dirt's arrest when he was in Biscaluz Recovery Center of Los Angeles County Jail and thus missed his court date
March 24, 2000	Dirt appeared in Los Angeles Superior Court apparently broken. He was sedate, disheveled, and obviously distraught. He admitted to violating probation and showed a completely different tone.
November 2000	While on the run, Dirt went into the studio with RZA to record. He also stopped by a Wu show to make a cameo appearance on stage, telling the stunned crowd, "I can't stay on stage too long; the cops is after me." A few days later, Dirt was signing autographs in a Philadelphia McDonald's parking lot when he was nabbed by police.
May 1, 2003	Released from prison and put on probation.

◇◇◇

With nine arrests in thirteen months, comedian Chris Rock joked that "ODB couldn't have committed all of those crimes himself. Coolio had to be responsible for some of that shit."

The crimes for which Russell Tyrone Jones had been convicted are widely documented and almost assuredly they are just a small fragment of the crimes he committed in total. His convicted crimes included but weren't limited to public drunkenness, urinating in public, disorderly conduct, and lewd behavior. As he was addicted to drugs later in life, he was addicted to the satisfaction of getting something for nothing, which he received as a small time shoplifter.

He received satisfaction from being catered to, but who doesn't? The difference, though, was that his sense of entitlement ballooned with his fame. He didn't care if he got caught or not. It made no difference to him because he had no plans of paying society back or anyone else.

The less Dirt gave a fuck, the more his public persona was elevated. The more his public persona was elevated, the more records he sold. And, of course, the more records he sold, the more money he made. Dirt's bad boy image could be measured by his bankroll.

What he couldn't see, however, was that his bottom line would be affected by his legal issues.

On the surface, this behavior may have seemed insignificant, but when Russell was stealing from convenience stores as a kid, it may have been an overlooked sign. Later as a substance-abusing adult who was caught trying to walk out of a Sneaker Stadium with a pair of size eleven Nikes, Dirt exhibited classic behaviors as an adolescent that led to later incidents in his life.

According to a study in the American Journal of Psychiatry in July of 2008 by a research team from Columbia University, there seems to be a direct correlation between shoplifting and alcoholism, shoplifting and bipolar disorder, shoplifting and a variety of antisocial behaviors.

The yearlong study found that the prevalence of lifetime shoplifting isn't all that uncommon; about eleven percent of the population. The large-scale survey revealed that shoplifting does, indeed, start early in life. Many people have stolen something in their lives or tried to get over on someone else. Regardless of how small the stolen article is, an individual's moral compass should prevent the act. For example, a lie is a lie regardless of how innocent it is. Crimes and lies should not be relative to the situation. They weren't to Dirt because they were meaningless to him.

According to the study, it was not morality that played the key role in if a person shoplifts or not. It is more about the feelings evoked from the act. How the person feels about getting the upper-hand is more of a predictor of life-long shoplifting than the age in which one shoplifts. Some offenders grow out of it. Some never do. People steal out of a sense of entitlement. Some out of spitefulness. Some, like Dirt, just thrive on getting over.

Dirt loved getting away with whatever he could. It was almost like a compulsion; impulsiveness; inner struggles of right and wrong take introspection. Dirt didn't have time for that. His impulsivity was almost child-like. He reacted and then thought.

◇◇◇

Dirt's immaturity was never more present as it was on January 10, 2000, when he appeared before the judge at Queens Criminal Court with an escort from the court-ordered rehabilitation facility, Impact House. Facing a charge of cocaine possession with intent to sell from an arrest the previous July, ODB was in the midst of a downward spiral caused by a staggering amount of legal issues. His legal issues were compounded by more arrests, hearings, and bad behavior.

He had a string of bad court room appearances nearly a year before, stemming from terroristic threats and breaking California's freshly instated bulletproof vest law. He gurgled chocolate milk on the stand, seemingly ignored the judge addressing him, and burst out into song in a jam packed elevator.

The year following that three-month trial, while he was in rehab in Carmel, NY, *Nigga Please* came out. The following winter of 2000, Dirt appeared in court. He was sullen, melancholy, and what appeared to be combative with his Impact House escort.

Leading up to this outrageous court appearance, Dirt dodged a murder charge for firing at a police officer who pulled his '99 Tahoe over for driving erratically and with the lights out.

When they searched his car, no weapon was found, but he ended up losing his license because of the stop. In the following month, March, he was arrested twice in less than a week when he was caught for driving without a license. He was also charged with possession with marijuana and three vials of crack were found in the vehicle. He told the arresting officer that he'd take the "marijuana charge," but asked, "Can you make the crack disappear?"

Another arrest was made in April when he ran a red light and this time he had twenty vials of crack with him. This is when he was sentenced to Impact House. In mid-October, he was two short months of finishing his rehab when he walked out of Impact House. Instead of going into hiding because he was violating a court order, Dirt joined The Wu on stage at the Hammerstein Ballroom in Manhattan. A few days later, he was recognized at a McDonald's and reported to Philadelphia police. He was captured and sent before Judge Joseph Grosso.

◇◇◇

On January 10 in Queens Criminal Court, Dirt had had enough of his counselor in his ear, trying to control his behavior. Witnesses said that Dirt and his counselor could be seen bickering and court officials, reporters, and lawyers all made note of the body language and apparent rift.

During the proceedings, Dirt was seen picking his nose, falling asleep, and saying stupid things like, "Do I make you horny?" when addressing the D.A. He even called the prosecutor a "sperm donor."

Upon leaving the courtroom, Dirt and the counselor went separate ways. Dirt apparently made a b-line to the liquor store, for when he landed in LA, he had a bottle in his possession. Impact House canned him from the program and Dirt was sent to Pasadena to complete a year of his sentence in a facility there.

On October 17, 2000, Dirt got into an argument with the staff at the rehabilitation center. He was tired of butting heads with the counselors; he knew that they really couldn't understand his particular plight, and he felt that none of it was helping him anyway. So, with two months left to serve out his court-ordered treatment, Dirt became a fugitive by defiantly walking out of the facility.

Where he floated around for a month before showing up onstage is a question no one particular person is able to answer. Dirt probably didn't know either because it is safe to assume that he spent most of the time drugged and drunk and hopping from bed to bed.

◇◇◇

Dirt selectively chose his friends by those who also liked to do drugs and were able to keep a secret. His heavy, hard-drug use seemed to come as a surprise to his business associates, who thought most of Dirt's persona was a shtick. The VP of Elektra, Beth Jacobson, told journalist William Shaw in a *Blender* interview, "At the time I was working with him, I didn't see any hard drugs."

Jacobson knew Dirt ever since RZA was shopping him around for the first album. She knew Dirt to use "only weed. And he liked to drink. Crack and dust, these are things I found out later he was dabbling in."

Jacobson also knew how outrageous and shocking Dirt could be. She told Shaw the story of a music-industry event that took place in a Miami night club. She related the story as evidence that Dirt needed someone to stop him, intervene, and say to him, "Listen, this shit is not going to fly," as she put it.

The music was loud and thumping and it was dark. With lights flickering, Dirt was able to catch Jacobson's eye from his table. He began waving her over.

When she approached, she found Dirt getting a blow job from a groupie. He was smiling and motioning as if to say, "Looky here." Jacobson was pissed. She stormed off.

Later that night, when Dirt had a quiet minute with Jacobson, he put his arm around her as if to apologize. "What the fuck was that?" She asked, "You though I would like that?" Dirt's excess is what really irked her, but she was unable to articulate it at the time.

"Ah, baby," he cooed, "I just wanted you to see how I could get my dick sucked, Electra-style."

In a weird kind of way, she was humored by the response and how he was kind of making sense. He was taking what was given to him and making no bones about it. It was an authentic response. Perhaps that is why no one intervened. To those that knew him and hung out with him, his excesses seemed genuinely appropriate. Jacobson believed that no one intervened (like she failed to do that night in Miami) because deep down "everyone was enjoying the show too much."

Dante Ross told Shaw for the *Blender* article, "To a lot of people who deem themselves politically correct—collegiate types—I think Dirty became their minstrel show. He was as close as they could get to the ghetto and watch someone totally dissolve as a human, while sitting far enough back to laugh."

So, again, it kind of made sense that Dirt would walk away from rehab and instead of someone convincing him to return to complete the program, it made sense that he should stay on the run and do as much drugs and drink as much alcohol as he could before he was caught and sent to jail.

◇◇◇

A few days before he was apprehended in Philly, he made a special appearance, and even this made sense in Dirt's world. To anybody else on the run from the law, appearing on stage would be out of the question, but to Dirt…

On November 21, 2000, The Wu was celebrating the release of their much anticipated album *The W*. Dirt, because he was in prison during the sessions, appeared on one track, "Conditioner," which also featured Snoop Dogg. The vocals were recorded through the telephones used for inmates to talk to visitors. It wasn't a prop, but it was a good gimmick. The song is all but forgotten today. The memorable track from the LP was "Gravel Pit," part of a time-travel trilogy of videos.

For the most part, the CD had a lukewarm reception by critics, yet the album was certified double platinum. Even though the crowd applauded on queue after the songs from the new album, the fans erupted when they launched into classic Wu songs. But there was something lacking that night at the Hammerstein Ballroom in front of a small crowd there by invitation only in the 4,000 capacity theater.

Hiding his face backstage and sneaking past security and the police with his entourage, Dirt made the night memorable. Even though reviews referred to the show lasting less than an hour and being pretty run-of-the-mill, it was a night to remember.

Starting the show late, RZA began hyping the fact that Dirt was there, teasing the crowd intermittently. He said, "I don't think ya'll understand what's going on here tonight." RZA wore a deep-brown leather bucket hat high on his head. The brim, with the underside in a contrasting beige, was turned up the whole way around. It matched his leather jacket. "This is the first time in three long years that all nine members of The Wu are all together."

The crowd understood exactly what RZA was alluding to, but they had to ask themselves how that could be. As far as they knew, Dirt was in rehab.

"Tonight will be the first time in three years," RZA said turning stage right. Just off stage, the curtain began to move, and Dirt slowly walked out from behind it as the single piano note from "Shimmy Shimmy Ya" began to sound. The fans exploded. That could only me one thing. Dirt was here!

Dirt walked out on stage with a black bottle of champagne. He looked overweight, but he looked damn good. He was wearing baggie black jeans and an oversized, blazing orange sweater that looked more like a parka. A large, black toboggan was pulled down to his eyes. He had his glasses on, which made him look like he just walked off of the campus of NYU.

After doing "Shimmy Shimmy Ya," Dirt said, "I'm gonna let all you niggas know something," he said addressing a predominately white, suburban crowd. "You know they had Ol' Dirty Bastard locked down, right?" There was a hiss from the crowd.

"Well, I'm here to tell ya' that they can't keep Ol' Dirty Bastard down. Now, I'm free!" The crowd cheered. "I'm free, and I'm out there like a bird flying around, so ya'll better leave some birdseed on your windowsills," (Dirt was back!) "because I may be flying by your house." The crowd cheered.

"You know," he went on, "that I'm still surviving on some shit like, just walking through, word is bond...RZA..." he searched for a single face to focus on, but they all merged together in one, Technicolor blur.

"RZA," Dirt continued, "RZA, I can't stay on stage tonight. The cops is after me," but Dirt stayed and did a couple of versus from two more songs before he disappeared backstage and out of the theater without being snatched up by authorities.

The media ate it up and Dirt's appearance gained national media coverage. Dirt's bad boy image and his apparent snubbing of the law was elevated to "folk hero" status by the media. Americans love the outlaws. The authorities made it clear that Dirt was on the run. There was an all points bulletin out for his arrest and anyone with knowledge of his whereabouts was to call the police.

Despite the pleas on the news, Dirt was able to dodge police, regardless of his unmistakable appearance.

◇◇◇

Six days later, Dirt was in a McDonald's drive-thru on the corner of S. 29th and Grey's Ferry Ave. in South Philadelphia in a blue 1991 Mitsubishi Galant with New Jersey license plates. When Dirt pulled over into a parking spot to eat, he was approached by a couple of fans who stopped to talk and ask for his autograph. Typically gracious to fans (when he felt like it), Dirt obliged and before anyone realized it, a small crowd of fans started gathering in the parking lot. The manager on duty noticed the disturbance and called the police, unsure as to what was really going on in the lot.

On patrol, Officer Rebecca Anderson and Officer Charlene Joyner answered the call and arrived at the McDonald's. The officers stopped to see what was going on and Dirt assumed that they, too, were fans seeking an autograph. When they approached Dirt, the two immediately recognized him. Anderson asked for I.D. Dirt gave her a phony I.D. from a check-cashing outlet that had a fake name on it, but he told them his real name when they asked him for it.

As E! Online reported, "The arresting officer knew it was him because her kid was a big fan," said a source close to Anderson. "ODB knew he was wanted and was basically nice about it."

Her superior, Sergeant Mel Williams of the Philadelphia Police, said, "She knew him from listening to his music and knew he was wanted by police. She stopped him and found out it was him. She then took him into custody without incident."

The New York Daily News, however, reported an entirely different episode two days later, one much more interesting. Detective Frank Wallace, investigating the case, corroborated that the officers were indeed "fans of his music, and they knew from media coverage that he's wanted. They were really interested to meet him," and that, "It was a neat experience for them."

But the fact that Dirt went peacefully and willingly during the arrest does not coincide with the story in *The NY Daily News.* They reported that Dirt tried to flee the scene by speeding off, but the cops quickly blocked the exits, pulled their guns, pulled his car over, and then and only then did he surrender peacefully.

◇◇◇

Dirt spent a few days in a Philadelphia holding cell before he was extradited back to New York. He was deemed a fugitive from justice and held without bail. He released a statement through his lawyer at the time, Robert Shapiro. He said, "The government is trying to kill me." The media gawked.

Perhaps a sly attempt for pity and showing Dirt's deteriorated mental state, Shapiro's released statement seemed a coded message that Dirt needed help. Not able to come out with the truth at the time because he was being paid to be Dirt's lawyer, Shapiro spoke out in 2008. The quote, "The government is trying to kill me," was lost in the static of ODBisms. True, there was a common belief that Dirt was unhinged, but there was always questions as to what extent. Should he be medicated? Institutionalized? Was he a danger to himself or others?

Shapiro told biographer, Jamie Lowe, that he did think that Dirt was mentally insane, a diagnoses of Paranoid Schizophrenia that went virtually untreated. Without pointing fingers, Shapiro alluded to warning signs.

Me gusta

God Made Dirt

◇◇◇

Dirt's story could be a tale about the ineffectiveness of the system's inability to deal with mentally ill patients who are drug addicts.

Dirt's behavior, whether drug induced or not, was beyond his control. In order for the system to rehabilitate Dirt, that was the simple fact that needed to be addressed. But, where do you start to help Dirt? The system couldn't answer this question, and his mother spent years looking for answers. How do you help Dirt? Cherry said on numerous occasions that she wanted to help Dirt, but didn't know how. She said that she spent sleepless nights crying out of worry.

◇◇◇

After many trial postponements and legal posturing, in April of 2001, Dirt accepted a deal that essentially expunged all other offenses in New York in exchange for a guilty plea to the cocaine possession charges. He received the minimum sentence of two to four years in prison, and he received credit for the eight months that he already served. He was also permitted to serve out the time that he owed California concurrently.

In July, before being sent to state prison, Dirt allegedly attempted suicide and was put on suicide watch. He was given a psychiatric evaluation, but the results were not made public, though apparently he was deemed fit to serve his sentence. When asked, his defense team made absolutely no statement and every paper reported that Dirt's attorneys were "unavailable for comment."

Dirt was sent to the Arthur Kill Correctional Facility in downstate New York. The fun, the drugs, the alcohol, the sex, the recording studio where he felt most useful, all came to an abrupt halt. Dirt's world came crashing down on him and everyone who knew him also knew that they had seen the real Ol' Dirty Bastard for the very last time. ODB was only 31, and he was already a dead-man-walking.

Interlude VI—ODB 101

As with any great poet or lyricist, Dirt's unorthodox street rhymes can be broken down as if they were classical forms of poetry. Dirt used poetic devices that can be analyzed in any literature class: similes, personifications, allusions, and metaphors.

The following is a brief introduction of the top four poetic devices in Ol' Dirty Bastard's lyrical style.

1) RZA and The Wu relied on **trochaic** verse in the early rhymes. Trochaic verse is when an accented syllable is followed by an unaccented syllable. It gives a regimented beat and rhythm. Take the example of "Shame on a Nigga." With a cadence established, Dirt would play off of that in his verses.

> Chorus key tag line:
> SHAME/ on/A/ nig/GA,
> WHO/ tries/ TO/ run/ GAME/ on/ A/ nig/GA

2) For humorous effect, ODB often used similes and metaphors. **Similes** are comparisons using "like" or "as" and **metaphors** are words or phrasing literally denoting an object or idea that is then applied to another more humorous item, usually sexually related in ODB's lyrics. The first few lines of his first verse of "Dog Shit" are a prime example:

> She flew in *like* calm breeze. [Simile]
> Tall brown skin, her weave *like* palm trees. [Simile]
> I went coconuts. [Metaphor]
> Dipped my Dunkin' between your Donut. [Metaphor]

The last line is also a great example of how Dirt used **alliteration** (repetition of beginning consonant sounds).

3) Part of Dirt's overall genius that was totally original and organic was his use of grunts and groans and mono-syllabic, guttural words and sounds. Poets use **onomatopoeia** (words to imitate sounds) for sound quality, but Dirt used it as a built-in beat-box in his verse. Consider all the great usage in "Brooklyn Zoo":

> I drop science like girls be dropping babies,
> Enough to make a nigga go cr-a-a-a-zy

-and-

> If you wanna step to my motherfuckin' wreck,
> (Ch-ch plow! plow! plow!) blown to death,
> You got shot cause you knock knock knock,
> "Who's there?" Another motherfuckin' hardrock,

4) **Assonance** is the refrain of vowel sounds to create internal rhyming within phrases or sentences and together with alliteration and consonance (repetition of beginning consonant sounds) serves as one of the building blocks of verse. Dirt's use of assonance added great sound quality to his rhymes. Here's an example from "Dirty the Moocher"

> All I wanna see is fire cause I'm makin shit hot
> Like the blow between glocks, mad niggas I shot
> Give a fuck on a cop, conversate with a lock
> Down at the chop-chop, 600th and Rock
> Crazy as a fox tryin to rob Fort Knox

6

Time Out

Life was hard for Russell Tyrone Jones on the inside. His Paranoid Schizophrenia told him that he was the target of guards and inmates and, at times, that seemed to be the case. Those who were there doing time obviously know the truth, but when Dirt was released and in front of the cameras for the VH1 show, his version is what stuck.

However, when biographer Jamie Lowe went through miles of red tape to talk to an inmate that did time with Dirt, she found in her interviews that no one could confirm his stories of being beaten by guards and harassed by his fellow inmates. Instead, it seemed as though Dirt was given rock star treatment. All the inmates obviously knew who he was since most were rap fans anyway. Sure, he may have been a pain in the ass to the COs on occasion, but they were fully aware of his status as an entertainer and his fragile mental state.

Even though Dirt sat rotting in prison, mind deteriorating, mental stability failing, he was able to release an album. Yes, an album. Panned by critics and found disappointing by fans because it mainly consisted of remixes and pieced together rhymes, *The Trials and Tribulations of Russell Jones* was released on March 19, 2002 by D3 Entertainment.

D3 Entertainment, a Los Angeles label and a division of their parent, Riviera label, seemed on a mission to scoop up Rap artists unable to get a deal. With limited distribution, they mainly attracted mid-level performers. They also laid claim to an awkward assortment of compilations, including such artists as Patsy Cline and Mel Torme, so it seemed as if their stable of artists were either dead, on their way up, or on their way down the ladder of success.

In fact, some don't even call *The Trials and Tribulations of Russell Jones* a legitimate release, but a compilation CD. Sure, Dirt's rhymes were present, but he really didn't seem to be. He had no say in the production and many of the songs consisted of lyrics from his other releases. Some of the lyrics were from old tracks lifted from *Return of the 36 Chambers: The Dirty Version, Nigga Please*, and even from *Wu-Tang Forever*. Other ad-libbing and verses were recorded before he was picked up at the McDonald's in Philly for another solo project that never came to fruition. RZA was stuck holding the material when Dirt spun helplessly out of control.

◇◇◇

While in "Little Siberia," what the Clinton Correctional Facility is nicknamed because of its remoteness on a New York hillside that borders Canada, Dirt grew further and further away from himself and he knew it, too.

Clinton has been a maximum security prison since 1845 and it is known to have broken such men as Lucky Luciano, Jesse Friedman, Hell Rell and Tu Pac Shakur. The facility can house two thousand nine hundred prisoners and all are dangerous criminals. Though Clinton housed some Five-Percenters, Dirt did not associate with any of them.

Touched by insanity and marred by emotional ineptness, he was in no condition to promote an album, but it seemed like a good gimmick, considering all the other outrageous materials that Dirt put out, including trailers of himself after a shit bizarrely staring at the camera as he unrolls his toilet paper.

Dirt had what he called "seldom" visitors since he was moved from Arthur Kill Correctional Facility because Clinton, in the town of Dennemora, is over three hundred and twenty miles from New York City. Cherry and

Icelene would take the kids to see Dirt in prison while he was in Arthur Kill, but making it to Clinton was "almost impossible."

◇◇◇

William Shaw from *Blender* was sent to Clinton to interview Dirt to cover the new release. Dirt, now known as Inmate 01-A-4392, was apparently oblivious to the arrangement. Shaw is a British journalist with no real distinguishing features. He knew of Dirt's background and he really didn't know what to expect from Dirt when he met him. However, what he found wasn't remotely what he expected. He made note of Dirt's appearance: "Hunched over…looking much older than a thirty three year old should…This ODB just looks sad, defeated, and nervous… He has acquired the habit of the prison underdog: Avoid eye contact at all costs."

When Shaw and Dirt were brought face to face in the visiting room, Dirt asked, "Who are you?"

Shaw reintroduced himself and told Dirt why he was there. Dirt tried to turn on his showbiz charm, but it wasn't there. Instead, he said, "Ah, my album? When's it coming out?"

"Yes, *your* album," Shaw answered, "I understand that it is due out in mid-March."

Dirt allowed it to register. "Well, what do you want to know?"

"For a start, how're things going in here?"

"Not too good," he sighed. "Not too good."

"How much have you changed since the days when you, GZA, and RZA first started performing together?" Shaw asked him.

Dirt took some time, reached down into his gut and faced a harsh reality. "I was a lot sharper then. I'm not so sharp now," ODB said sadly as if he were describing someone he barely knew. "It's like somebody's put the kitchen implement up on the shelf, if you know what I mean."

He continued talking, trying to get down to the heart of the matter. His thoughts were a jumbled mess and he wanted Shaw to make the most sense out of them. "It's not easy for me," he says miserably, "I feel like I'm in a spaceship that has just landed here. And when you get out, you realize there's nothin' there at all. I don't know." He took a moment to pause and collect more thoughts. "This is a corrupt facility," he said, glancing nervously to his left where two guards stood watching over the interview. "In here, there's people in here that are corrupt."

At a holding facility in New York, Dirt suffered a broken leg when he was assaulted by other inmates. Seizing on the opportunity, Shaw asked him what had happened during the incident.

"What happened?" ODB repeated, "I was in a fight." He left it at that, but Shaw waited to make sure that Dirt wasn't going to elaborate on the event. He refused to say more about it.

"What do you do with your time all day?" Shaw asked, knowing that a creative mind like Dirt's must be tortured in an "ugly, bleak" facility like Clinton, which was known to house some of the hardest, scariest criminals in the state of New York.

"Every morning, I go to drug rehabilitation class. The rest of the time I just spend in my cell." Dirt's cell is small, so he doesn't have to share it with anyone. He was thankful for that.

"Have you made any friends here?"

"Friends?" he snorted as if the question were ridiculous. "No, I don't have any friends in here."

"You keep to yourself then?"

"Oh, yes," he said flatly. "I don't mix with other people."

"So what do you do here?" Shaw asked still trying to get some answers as to how Dirt existed in such a restrictive environment.

"Watch TV."

"Are you learning anything from the rehab class?"

"Not really."

"You turned thirty three two weeks ago. What did you do?"

"I didn't do much. Watch TV."

"Not your favorite birthday?"

Dirt smiled. Even he could see the humor in the question. "No," he answered, "Not the best. There ain't much good on TV."

Given this rare opportunity to talk to Dirt behind bars, Shaw wanted to get him to clarify another incident that took place in July 2001. Reporters made mention of some bandages on Dirt's left wrist, perhaps evidence of a suicide attempt. His attorney at the time, Peter Frankel, released a statement, insisting that the rumors were blown out of proportion. The statement said that the bandages were "in a location that would not be consistent with the suggestion that there was a suicide attempt," but that didn't allay the rumor.

"When you were in prison last summer," Shaw began, "people were concerned about your mental health. You were reportedly kept on suicide watch."

ODB seemed distant, fixating on a spot on the table in front of him. "I think things are a lot worse with me now," he said.

"Your state of mind is worse?"

"Yes."

"Do you take any medication?"

"No," he answered while shaking his head. "I don't. You have to keep your eyes open here, so you can't take anything. This isn't a place where you would want to not know what was going on. This place," he was still shaking his head, "it's full of convicts."

Shaw was about to ask another question and move the interview along, but he could tell that Dirt wanted to say more. Shaw picked up on it and was about to goad him when Dirt started, "You know," he said,

"I don't know whether Ol' Dirty Bastard is even here anymore." He continued focusing on that imaginary spot on the long, institutional table. "I think he's gone."

Shaw lightened the conversation by focusing on the future and the new album about to drop. He gave Dirt the list of names that were also featured on the album, Insane Clown Posse, Too Short, E-40, C-Murder, and his long time friend, Buddha Monk, just to name a few.

"E-40 is on there?" Dirt brightened. "He has the same birthday as me."

Shaw went on to describe for Dirt the cover art on the CD that the label had sent to the magazine as a promo. It was a simple close-up of a young Ol' Dirty Bastard with his eyes clear and wide.

"Ah, right," Dirt said showing the most interest in Shaw and the interview since it began. "Can I see it?"

"No, sir, I'm sorry," Shaw disappointedly reported. "I was forbidden to bring anything in, but I can give you a number of someone you can talk to. I can bring his card to you tomorrow, if you'd like."

"Sure, man, I'd like to see that," Dirt said, and the two shook hands.

Shaw had a positive feeling about how the visit ended. He wrote, "ODB seems pleased to have had the chance to talk—especially about the world outside his cell." Yet when he went back to the prison and waited an extraordinary amount of time in the waiting room, a guard appeared instead of Dirt. "I'm sorry," the guard said, "He's refusing the visit."

Shaw asked the guard to relay the message that they could meet again the next morning and that he did indeed have the number of someone who could help Dirt. But once again, Dirt refused to come out of his cell.

Shaw's piece, "This Man Desperately Needs Help" ran the Friday before the LP hit the streets. In the article, Shaw accounted for how D3 was able to pen the deal with Dirt. When Elektra dropped Dirt, Bo Glasper, his manager, pitched the idea to D3's founder, Aldy Damien, who went ahead and put a deal together for a new Ol' Dirty Bastard LP. "In return for an undisclosed advance paid to Icelene, Glasper and Wu-Tang leader

RZA supplied D3 with previous ODB recordings—many just snippets or half-recorded tracks. Damian also paid to use The Wu-Tang logo on the CD's sleeve," Shaw wrote in the article.

Even though D3 created what little buzz they could for the release with their limited budget, album sales for the record were poor probably for a host of reasons, but mostly because it was lambasted by critics as being a "shoddy piece of exploitation." Even MTV, an outlet that basically launched Dirt's career through gimmicks like the welfare-in-a-limo visit, turned their back on the project. Dirt didn't monitor sales, not that he ever did. But since he had no control over his bank account from prison, he couldn't see how sales were affecting it, like he could in the past.

Otherwise, on the inside, Dirt waited for time to pass and kept track of the days only by the programs on TV. Also, as he said in the *Dirty Minded Documentary*, he spent a lot of the time masturbating. He said, "Everyday, like probably three times a day, I'd jerk my dick off so much that the prisoners would say 'Yo! Ol' Dirty, chill the fuck out!' Every girl I saw on T.V., her ass looked funny to me and I just kept jerkin' my dick off, every fuckin' day and night."

7

The Press Conference (Remix)

Russell Tyrone Jones appeared in front of the New York's parole board on February 3, 2003 a broken man. Dressed in greens, Dirt walked into the room, head down, eyes on the floor. It was a far cry from the Dirt that walked into the courtroom with contempt and complacency. He was serious. Focused. To him, he was fighting for his life because he felt that he was going to end up dead if he stayed in jail. For almost two and a half years, Dirt's world came to a screeching halt and time slipped away behind bars.

As time slipped away, so did much of what made Ol' Dirty Bastard who he was. There was no way at this point that Dirt could go the way that his father always wanted, work hard, stay clean, and grow old quietly and comfortably. He would have to start from scratch and tap into the JobCorp training of his youth. Keeping a daily nine-to-five never seemed like a workable solution.

But there he was, facing Commissioner W. William Smith, Jr. and Commissioner William Crowe in the battle for his life. Also present in representing the Division of Parole was Warren Mason, Facility Parole Officer 1 and Ron Meier, Facility Parole Officer.

Before facing the parole board, Dirt gave copies of CDs that he made to the commissioners to evaluate his abilities to make a living for himself after prison. The board was also aware that Dirt had a $500,000 record deal waiting for him at the end of the prison yard.

In seeing how fragile Dirt was and how vulnerable that he would be upon leaving prison, there were certain needs that the board wanted to make sure that were met. There was a concern that Dirt was going to go back to his old ways without any type of support or safety net. There needed to be a change and they knew deep in their hearts that prison couldn't make the possible change for Dirt. He had to do it. If they couldn't see what changes were necessary, there was a good chance that the commissioners would deny release.

The first questions that they asked detailed where Dirt was going to stay and if he was willing to "change from what your past was."

"Yes," Dirt answered.

"Do you know what I am talking about?" Commissioner Smith asked.

"Yes."

"I don't know if that is the fast life or what. Drugs will equal prison, right?" The commissioner asked.

"Yeah," Dirt replied. "It was the fat life making records, making a lot of money. For a kid that never made any money, it tends to get…you know…" Dirt searched for the words to articulate how corrupted his life became from what he saw as easy money. And it was easy for him. Hanging out in studios. Partying. Getting noticed. It all came so naturally in the early 90s that money to give away was just gravy. "I am a kid," Dirt said, "I have a lot of money and I am not used to it, you know what I'm sayin'?" The emotion was there but the words weren't.

"Look where you ended up, where you are sitting right now," said the Commissioner in hopes of getting Dirt to see at least one more time how his life could end up right back there in front of the board.

Commissioner Crowe wanted to know, "Do you have any of that money left?"

"Yeah, I do. I just came out," Dirt stammered, "one of those records was just made last April," he finished.

"How much money do you have, approximately? Do you have enough to cover your home?"

"No," Dirt bowed his head low.

"Okay. Do you have to work?"

"Yes."

"You may have to sell your home or whatever, who knows?"

"Yeah, if I don't get out, I am going to have to sell my home," Dirt said pleadingly, but with a hint of firmness.

"You may have to even if you get out," the Commissioner said to get a reaction from Dirt.

"No," Dirt said with some defiance. "Not at all."

"What is the mortgage a month?"

"The mortgage a month is fifteen hundred dollars." In an attempt to redirect the hearing and this particular line of questioning that was making him nervous, Dirt begged, "Can I tell you something, Sir?"

When he was granted permission to speak, Dirt explained that he had a record deal and that he was, indeed, going back to work to do the only thing that he really knew how to do well. His work was in the studio and a prime opportunity was waiting for him to jumpstart his life and revive his career. He wanted to be back in the studio.

"Where is that?" the Commissioner asked.

"In Manhattan," Dirt answered.

"The reason I asked those questions," Commissioner Crowe started, "I don't know where the studio was, if you had plans to leave the State. You understand that if we release you now on your conditional release date in July, that is the conditional release date that we show now, no matter when you leave, you have to report to your parole officer. You have not been on parole before. You have to report to your parole officer. You absolutely cannot leave the state. Do you understand?"

"Yes, sir," Dirt meekly answered.

The parole board went on the attack. They reminded Dirt that he was not a model citizen even behind prison walls. They brought up charges from the COs that Dirt once flooded his cell and set fire to his mattress. They wanted him to question his own sanity. They wanted him to see the "difficulties" that he would pose on society.

"No, I didn't flood my cell," Dirt protested.

They knew from past instances that Dirt was prone to tell a lie. The commissioners persisted, "Did you set something on fire?"

"No, I had my cigarette burning," he faltered. "Okay," he started, "what happened, one time I had my cigarette burning, and I fell asleep with it burning."

Dirt's response was slurred. His teeth and tongue kept getting in the way of his clarity. "I didn't hear the word," a commissioner said. "Seat?"

"No, I fell asleep."

"Did it set the bedclothes on fire?

"It burned a little hole in my sheet, not my mattress."

"Okay, so the bedding. And you understand the seriousness of that?"

"Yes, I do."

"You are in a structured environment here, among other things. I know that you had a number of Tier IIs, which are lesser disciplinary reports, but you have had two Tier IIIs, is that right?"

"Yes, sir," Dirt cowered.

The commissioner talked down to Dirt and showed the authority that was needed to keep Dirt in line. He reminded Dirt that he had been disciplined for behavior, stripped of freedoms, and docked "good time of three months."

"They didn't take away my good time," Dirt corrected.

"They haven't yet. They could in the future, right?"

"No, they got up to five or six months to do that and it is past already."

"Well, that may be your understanding."

"Yes," Dirt conceded, "maybe my understanding, yes."

"But they still can," the commissioner continued, "They can look at you, the Time and Allowance Committee, and see what would happen. There is three months loss of recommended good time. There is only a single Tier III. There is bribery, extortion, three months recommended good time. That happened about a year ago. You were in Clinton?"

"Yes."

"What happened there?"

"Okay, this is what happened, like this: I was going to school and teacher, he knew who I was. He knew that I was a rap star. One day, he asked me for an autograph for his children. I said, 'okay, I will sign your autograph, no problem.' Next few days later, he told me that he wrote a ticket on me stating that I tried to rob him for an autograph and I was saying, 'Why would I bother anybody for an autograph?' For what happened, I was in the wrong place at the wrong time. I'm not saying that I was not wrong, but I was not wrong because he asked me for an autograph for his children."

The board was confused by Dirt's story. One asked, "This had to do with him touching you some kind of way in your sternum, right?"

"Yeah," Dirt answered.

"I have to tell you," Commissioner Smith said while shaking his head, shrugging his shoulders, and gesturing over the table with his hands, "I have no clue who you are beyond these things sitting in front of me, beyond those CDs, which I call records, shows how much I pay attention. I don't know who you are. I don't like rap music; that doesn't tell me anything. What you are telling me happened inside State prison and has to do with your fame. Maybe that tells you something."

Checking Dirt's safety net, they asked about the people that he associated with. His attorney, Robert Shapiro, his entourage, RZA, The Wu, and others were brought into question. "Do they give you good advice?" They asked. Dirt said that they did. "Did your mother ever have any trouble with the law? They asked. Dirt said that she hadn't. "Do you have any brothers or sisters?"

"I am the only one in my whole family that ever had trouble with the law. Me. Myself. I have eight brothers and sisters."

"Not one of them has been to state prison? What do they do for a living?"

"Not one of them. My sister, she is a toll booth clerk. My other sister, she goes to college. My brother has a degree in music—he has a Master's Degree in music. My other brother, he is now in the Marines. He's in Japan now in the Marines. My other little sister, one of my little sisters, I just got her a job."

"And of all those children, all those siblings, who do you think your mother has had to shed the most tears for?"

"Me, of course," Dirt flatly said.

"Well, so that is all I'm saying. I am not going to go through anymore, but you need to pay attention."

"Yes, I do." Without thinking and because it seemed like the right thing to say, Dirt said, "I am sorry, Sir."

"Sorry," the commissioner almost scoffed, "that is all fine and dandy. You don't have to be sorry to me. You need to obey the law. Stay away from drugs and not do other crimes. That is what you need to do. It is a lot more honorable to be a toll booth collector where they check you every day that you are not five dollars short and go home and be honest instead of going home and doing what you did."

Dirt couldn't help but think that he was being lectured once again by his father, William. It was the very same lesson, and, apparently, it worked because Dirt's other family members all followed that path. But not him.

Was he stubborn? Was he belligerent and evil? Or, was he just bored easily, and once he's bored…

"What do you mean?" Dirt asked. "The drug thing?"

"Yes," the commissioner answered. The board began asking questions about Dirt's other various offenses: The bullet proof vest; Missing court dates; Drug arrests. After quite some time, the commissioner asked, "When was the last time you did drugs?"

"It has been almost four years now," Dirt replied.

The board knew that Dirt was either lying or that he had lost track of time. The timeline didn't add up. Yes, he had been in and out of rehab leading up to prison, but he had only spent two years in prison up to this point. "Is that the longest you have ever gone in your adult life without drugs?"

"Yes, I'm sorry," he said again. "I did the crime, Sir, you know. I was young. I was foolish, foolish thinking, Sir. That day I just bought a new car. I bought a Mercedes Benz and, like I said, I was young. I didn't know better, you know? When you got the stardom, you got the ladies all around. You got all kinds of foolish things messing with your head."

Commissioner Crowe agreed, "There is a lot of temptation out there. And the lifestyle that you have been successful in, there is even more because you are a celebrity, if I can use the term. And people want to be around celebrities and there is a lot of women and drugs and alcohol and partying and what you would call the 'fast life.'" Dirt agreed, nodding his head and thinking that someone finally understood his plight, yet Commissioner Crowe turned on him. "But, you know the difference between right and wrong and you know that drugs are illegal, but when you are partying, it is fun to get high, yet it is not worth the price, is it?"

"No, it is not. Not at all."

"The question that we have as Commissioners is what the future is going to hold for you? You have the ability, perhaps, to become a celebrity again and the advantage to you and your family is that you can make a very handsome living in that regard. The disadvantage is the strong influence from the women, the partying, the drugs, the alcohol, everybody that wants a piece of you."

"I learned from that," Dirt said, "No more of that."

"And you have to decide when you make your choices, is it worth it to you to come back into state prison behind bars with the green suit on and be denied your freedom and not be able to see your family, see your Mom, see your kids? Those are choices you and only you make."

"Yes, Sir," Dirt said almost testifying as if he were in church.

"Do you think that you, at this point in your life, can make the right decision?"

"Yes, Sir. I do believe so, yes, Sir. Prison taught me that I have children and my children is fifteen years old now and it doesn't look right to me, ya' nih' mean?"

"Is this a place for their father to be?" Commissioner Crowe asked.

"No, it is not," Dirt said.

"You are here for your own actions?"

"That is right. I am."

Satisfied, Commissioner Crowe turned it over to Commissioner Smith to give the final statements and to finalize and adjourn the hearing. "We are going to consider what you told us. We are going to look at all the factors considered by law, certainly the record in front of us. We have letters from the defense attorney and district attorney we have read. One way or another, in the not too distant future, you will be in the community. You talked about your conditional release date. You have a period of time that you will be on supervision until approximately November 2004, so, whether we get you into the community a few months earlier, you would continue to be monitored and assisted by our parole officer. That is kind of what we are going to look at, Commissioner Crowe and myself. We have asked a lot of questions. Is there anything else that you want to say before we end?"

This was Dirt's chance. There was a big build up as if he was going to say something very profound, like in a movie when the defendant gets up, spills his guts, and endears himself to his critics and counterparts. The crowd cheers. The credits come down, and the lights go up.

"I just want to say I'm thankful to be here at the board and everything because the crime that I did, it was wrong. And I feel that I paid for it for being in prison because I've never been in prison before and prison is a scary place for a man to be. I learned my lesson. I learned a valuable lesson, Sir." There were no cheers.

"Alright."

"And, like I said," Dirt tried again, "I got a job outside now and a record company just offered me $500,000 and if I can get out, I don't know if in the future it is still going to be there. In July, I don't know if it is going to still be there. I know now it is there, you know, and I was just bringing that to your attention so I can take care of my family.

"I'm not so concerned about that," Commissioner Smith flatly stated. "There is almost a part of me…I mean, you need to make a living, but there would almost be some comfort if I knew you were going to be making $500 a week rather than some other large amount, but we are not going to hold that against you. I am just saying that too much money, in some manner, contributed, but we are going to listen to your comments and listen to what you said."

And with that the parole board hearing came to an end.

Four months later, Dirt walked out of prison a free man. Well, almost free. Like the commissioner said, he had to check in regularly with his P.O. and he had to submit to random drug testing.

◇◇◇

The plan was for Dirt to stay with his mother, Cherry, and she was to offer the stability that the board was hoping for. Everyone with a vested interest in Dirt's release was ecstatic because the May release gave them plenty of time to iron out any details before the July first date that seemed arbitrarily made up. But was it arbitrary?

When Dirt was pitching the record contract to the parole board, there was no mention of the VH1 show, *ODB on Parole.* On one hand, the show seemed like a good way to monitor Dirt's behavior. In other respects, it was demoralizing for Dirt.

Immediately after Dirt's release, there was a whirlwind of activity. Lights, camera, action!

Damon Dash was on the curb and the two caught hands to pull each other closer for a slap on the back. Dash didn't look like your ordinary millionaire mogul. Hat turned sideways, baggie clothes, gold chain with a medallion, Dash was made for Hip Hop. He'd been out hyping Dirt's signing and much more was scheduled while the iron was hot. But, was Dirt ready? That was the question that the parole board and deep down Dash, Cherry, Icelene, and everyone else who knew Russell Tyrone Jones asked.

Once again, before he could even catch his breath with fresh air blowing in his face for the first time in over two years, Dirt was thrust into the spotlight at the center of attention. A microphone boom was dodging in and out of his face. A chiseled smile was spread across his face. His grin was so wide and cheeks so chubby that he looked younger; though the missing teeth and a peg where a cap was gave an indication to his hardness.

"Oh, man! Everyone's here!" he said as if he'd just been ambushed. "Even my aunt's here!" His eyes darted from face to face and Dash stepped aside so that Dirt could soak up the warmth from family members that he hadn't seen in years. After all of the hugs and greetings, Dirt was whisked away in a limo with an entourage. Cameras rolling and following his every move, Dirt looked shell shocked, but the smile stayed plastered to his face. "Where are we going?" He asked like a child thrown into his car seat, fully aware that he had no control over where the car was headed.

"Your press conference," Cherry answered.

"My what?" He was confused. He fought the urge to get pissed off. He kept smiling with his fucked up grill, but Cherry sensed his annoyance.

She, of course, had seen his temper. She also knew that he wouldn't blow his image in front of the camera so quickly.

"Your press conference. It's all for you," she cajoled. "We're headed there now."

"When'd all this happen?" Dirt asked.

"It's all been taken care of," she said. "Just be yourself and everything will be all right."

"Hey, Jarred. Jarred," Dirt said trying to get Weisfeld's attention over all of the females cackling in the limo. "Wha…I mean…Damon, man… what was that? What was Damon doing there?" Not used to being in front of the camera, he was as innocuous as he could be.

Weisfeld played it just as cool. "He just wanted to be there to see you."

The mix of friends laughing had caught up with Dirt, who seemed like he'd rather be back in his cell than on his way to a press conference. Then the cameras clicked off.

◇◇◇

By the time he arrived at the hotel and stepped out for the cameras once again, Dirt looked different. He looked transformed into his old self. At the press conference, Dirt accepted the fact that fame had put a sneak attack on him once again. He was over-stimulated, but he was ready for the cameras the second time around. So much had just been thrown at him that he was afraid to blink.

Ex-prisoners and drug addicts talk about how fast their worlds are when they are faced with the pace of life sober and on the outside. Ironically, though, even though the world is pushed into fast forward by being awake and a participant of life, they are still desperately bored. Dirt's mental illness manifested itself into creative energy. Along with the drugs and alcohol that made life more bearable, it seemed almost inevitable that he go back to drugs and possibly prison, but the ultimate catastrophe is what lay in waiting for Dirt.

Jarred Wiesfeld had Dirt's look and wardrobe already planned out. Dirt was to promote his new line of Rap wear and the idea was to profit from merchandising, just like The Wu had done and was still doing and just like Damon Dash was doing with Roc-A-Wear.

Along with Rap music, Dirt would be selling the Rap lifestyle. In order to live the lifestyle, kids had to buy the clothing.

At the press conference, Dirt was to wear a hooded, velour sweat suit jacket with "Dirt 718" on the back. Down the line, what Dirt wore on camera became an issue of contention. For one interview, Dash gave Dirt a Roc-A-Wear shirt to wear on camera when Weisfeld threw a fit. All of it was caught on camera and incorporated into the pilot episode, and it gave the impression that Weisfeld was going to be able to put up a good fight when needed.

Dirt, however, wasn't willing to fight over wardrobe. "That shit is so small and insignificant to me," he told Jarred, but Wiesfield knew the significance of getting face time with Dirt McGirt wear on camera. Perhaps Dirt overlooked the importance. Regardless, Weisfeld backed off and placated Dirt. Eventually though, Jarred persuaded him to wear Dirt McGirt wear instead of the Roc-A-Wear gear.

◇◇◇

If there was any doubt that prison had changed Dirt, it was confirmed at the press conference. He was the same ol' Dirty, though he insisted that he had a new name and a new attitude.

Dirt ranted about the police. He babbled and slurred his speech. He hit on reporters and cursed inappropriately. He seemed to piss away his one and only chance to make a new first impression.

To bystanders, it seemed like a disaster. But to others, it was pure gold. Ol' Dirty Bastard had a history of selling records as an outrageous Rap clown. Ol' Dirty Bastard was back.

Interlude VII—Prison

In a prison visiting room, sounds of steel doors clang shut. Other families are visiting inmates in forest green jumpsuits. Dirt sits with his back to a concrete block wall. Facing him across from a long table is his mother and Jarred Wiesfeld, a tall, lean twenty three year old.

JARRED:	Do you know why I'm here, Dirt?
DIRT:	Yeah, they say you was talkin' about some sort of TV show.
CHERRY:	Jarred's got a great opportunity for you, Rusty.
DIRT:	Well, how'm I gonna get the fuck outta here?
CHERRY:	That's the beauty of it, baby. The show is called *ODB on Parole*. It's a reality show. It will be all about you getting your life back on track. A big comeback.
DIRT:	Whatever it takes, Momma. I'm dyin' in this mothafucka. They gonna kill me up in this bitch.
CHERRY:	I know, baby. It pains me to see you in here like this and you're so far I can't even see you. You know I cry and pray for you every night, dontcha, Rusty? But hang in there. Jarred and I are gonna get you outta here.
DIRT:	Who's Jarred?
JARRED:	I'm Jarred. I contacted your mother because I got this great idea for a show, and your mother and I -
DIRT:	Whatever it takes, man. Whatever it takes to get me outta this mothafucka 'fore I end up dead.
JARED:	Then we can fill you in on the details later. I can have your mother sign the papers, and-
DIRT:	One condition, dude.

JARED:	What's that, Dirt?
DIRT:	Well, two conditions. The first one is get me outta this mothafucka. And the second one is that I'm gonna need a manager. Everybody left me and dumped me in this mothafucka, so I'm gonna need a manager. I'll do your show, but you gotta be my manager.
JARRED:	Big things are going to be happening for you, Dirt. You have two deals on the table. A record deal, and a clothing line. I've only been working as a production assistant at VH1. You might-
DIRT:	Then, no deal, man.
CHERRY:	Jarred? Dirt? Baby, maybe he's right, Rusty, because big things are about to happen. Maybe someone with a little more experience?
DIRT:	Look at this guy. I trust this guy. If he ain't gonna be my manager, then fuck the deal. I ain't ready for all that bullshit anyway.
JARRED:	Alright Dirt. You got a deal. I'll be your manager. But first, I'll get your Mom to be-
DIRT:	Fuck all that, Jarred. Just get me outta this mothafucka. A nigga don't stand a chance in here. They gonna kill me up in this bitch.

8

The Outro

There were signs that the end was near for Russell Tyrone Jones, but everyone chose to ignore them.

Buddha Monk, a good friend and stage mate, has been quoted as saying that in the last months leading up to Dirt's death that he would divvy drugs out to Dirt to keep him from overdosing. Dirt could lose track of how many drugs he was doing at once. He was like a puppy that would consume massive amounts of water, too immature to know when enough was too much.

Dirt found living with his mother to be stifling, although he was an admitted Momma's boy. The constant attention of the cameras was smothering. Financially, he needed her and her guidance to survive. Gigs had all but dried up because of his bad reputation for causing problems since the days of The Wu. His negative reputation grew like an untreated mold until he was deemed Public Enemy Number One among promoters and music execs.

Nobody was calling to collaborate with Dirt like the days of easy money when Dirt could earn up to $30,000 for a half day's worth of recording. Labels saw him as a liability; a risk not worth the effort.

But Dirt needed the money. His medications, sedatives, and anti-psychotic pills were costly, and performing was basically all that Dirt could do. Like a washed up boxer taking any fight that he could, Dirt's management team had to take whatever came down the pike to keep Dirt working. There were many people depending on him, and there was money to be made if Dirt could keep it together during brief appearances; however, this became more and more difficult for him to pull off.

A prime example is the night at the Knitting Factory. It was October 24, 2003 and Dirt was headlining for the Death Metal band Dillenger Escape Planet. It may not have made sense to see the two contrasting acts on the same bill, but when one considers the audience, white suburbanites visiting Brooklyn, it made perfectly good sense.

After the performance, the audience was dismayed by what took place. As concert reviewer Ryan S. Henriquez wrote for gloriousnoise.com, "Forget seeing Dirty. Tonight, I felt dirty. No, not in the way Rap fanatics talk about understanding or 'feeling' an artist, I mean I actually felt dirty—disgusting even. Bullfight dirty. Tampa strip club dirty. Tonight's performer was the shadow of a man catatonically sedated while parading on stage like the Elephant Man by his handlers and hangers-on."

Others who were there, including Jamie Lowe, described a night of debauchery: "A horrific and tragic display of the dark side of human existence that started at about two o'clock AM at the Knitting Factory in Brooklyn."

After some dead time after DEP's opening set, Sunz of Man and Brooklyn Zoo (Wu affiliates) took the stage and started hyping the crowd. Like the days of old, there were always plenty of performers on stage milling about. The fans were oblivious as to who these Rap groups were, but they played along, even though it was already very late.

"Where all my Brooklyn Zoo niggas at?" someone belted into the mic starting to hype the crowd. "Give that Dirty mothafucka a warm welcome!"

"Hold up, hold up, hold up," another cut in. "Turn the muthafuckin' mics up! Turn the mics up, man!"

"Yo, yo, yo," one shouted, "Big ups to Momma Wu. Momma Wu, we love you." Momma Wu stood off stage dressed to the nines.

"Peace to all my niggas."

"Word is bond. Peace an' unity to all y'all niggas."

As the troupe of rappers paced and milled around on stage, attempting to work the crowd into a "Wu-Tang" chant and failing miserably, a voice drowned out all the others. It was Dirt. It was that unmistakable voice that no one could imitate. That style that no one could bite.

The concert started to jump off, but when the owner of the voice appeared from behind the curtain, it was Buddha Monk, covering for a missing Ol' Dirty Bastard. Hernandez wrote, "Midway through the first song, ODB finally walked on stage, somehow to little fanfare. Most of the uninitiated crowd ('Is that him? Is that him?') did not even recognize him and why would they? This was not some grand entrance, but a meek hobbling steadied at both arms and assisted onto the stage by two handlers."

Scanning the crowd in a drug induced haze, Dirt made no attempt to rap. Instead, he appeared somewhat catatonic. Occasionally, he'd try to rap, but he'd miss his entry and/or slur and muddle his lines. They would have to have his raps queued up and served on a platter by another rapper, have his raps finished off by other rappers, or he would have to be just covered altogether by another rapper. To make matters worse, the DJ was playing not instrumentals but Dirt's original, vocal-led backing tracks.

During "Shimmy Shimmy Ya," Dirt dropped his mic. He made no effort to pick it up, but someone else picked it up for him and placed it into his hand with a smile. At one point, the crowd grew bored and restless, so they started entertaining each other by crowd surfing. One surfer was welcomed onto the stage, but then he was violently pummeled when he reached it.

At another point, in a feeble effort to enliven the crowd and dig even deeper into the pit, the only female on the stage began grinding on a rapper while exposing her breasts.

Between songs, Dirt mindlessly swayed to songs in his head. Buddha tried to work with the crowd and bring Dirt into the show. "Dirt, I

don't want you to do NOTHIN'. I want them to feel the VIIIIIIBE."
Turning to the audience, he said, "In order to be like we be, you got to
be… HIIIIIGH."

"Brooklyn Zoo" started cranking up, and Dirt was able to put in an entire
verse by himself, though his delivery was robotic and over-rehearsed. A
hint of a smile was noticed by Hernadez.

Other rappers took over the rest of "Brooklyn Zoo." The crowd began
to grow tired of the night's side-show charade and they began to boo.
Lowe, who wrote of being in the front row, said that she saw Dirt start
wailing. Tears streamed down his cheeks as he struggled to meander
around in his mind looking for the words to his signature song that he'd
done hundreds, if not thousands, of times. He was completely broken.
Toast. Done. He cried until he was helped off stage during his swan
song, "Brooklyn Zoo" in his old stomping ground, Brooklyn.

After a total of about thirty minutes, the show ended. Just like that. No
encore. No explanation. No nothing.

After that night, Damon Dash began feeling uneasy about his invest-
ment of time and money into Dirt. He altered the info on his website
concerning Dirt and eliminated dates, his bio, his features and his press
releases. Dirt seemed to be shelved to see where he was headed. The same
way other labels put Dirt on waivers before they canned him altogether,
Dash put the project into "wait-and-see" mode.

VH1 also became gun shy, perhaps coming to their senses, perhaps to
protect their interests. The show's pilot was shot, but no more shooting
was scheduled.

Speculating on Dirt's future, Hernandez foresaw Dirt babbling in his
old age like Ozzy Osborne, or he saw that Dirt might end up like Mike
Tyson, financially ruined, yet able to resurrect his career periodically
because people love the "spectacle of the maniac in the flesh." He wrote,
"But we all know better. Like Mike Tyson, Ol' Dirty Bastard's tale won't
have a happy ending. Something tells me that unlike Ozzy's, ODB's
handlers won't be competing for daytime Nielsens with Oprah and Ellen
anytime soon nor will they have the business savvy that comes with it.

Instead, they'll just be picking his pockets. At least, the mark won't be coherent enough to notice or care."

◇◇◇

Russell Tyrone Jones knew that his time was limited. He was depressed and morose. He was abusing drugs (in any form) and alcohol, and he morbidly talked about his death routinely. So when he told his mother that he would never see her again, she didn't pay him much attention. She has said on numerous occasions in various interviews that the last time she saw her son, he had properly said goodbye to her.

There is an internet rumor circulating about the events that led to ODB's death. Only those present know what really happened, and so far, they haven't revealed any details.

Some say that Dirt had panicked when he heard that the police were on their way to the Manhattan studio where he was recording for the upcoming album. In his haste to hide his bag of coke, he swallowed it. He had already taken some of the painkillers earlier before the session, some Tramadol. The coroner's report confirmed that a bag of coke was found in his stomach.

Interlude VII—RZA's Eulogy

RZA's Eulogy delivered at Dirt's funeral at St. James Presbyterian Church in Harlem was as follows:

Peace. My name is the RZA and we come to honor ODB, known to us as Russell Jones. At around the age of 13 or 14, we took a big interest in the Light, and we started reading books; and he took the name for himself, Ason Unique. He is a son who is unique.

When I look at his Momma Wu, Cherry, I was at their house all the time and I would spend weekends at their house. They were the only family that I saw as a family growing up. You see, Cherry would get up in the morning and make us pancakes. They'd have like two boxes of cereal in the cabinet. Uncle Wu, hard working man, both his parents worked, and they were a great example of a family. Ason Unique was a unique son from that family.

Ason Unique always had his different ways about him. He'd kick it at my neighborhood, and everybody was always like, "Hey, where's your cousin? Where's your cousin; he's so cool?" Everybody loved him. Everybody always wanted to be with him. Everywhere he went, people fell in love with him immediately.

But as time went on and we started going through life and we started going through the tribulations that we started going through as teenagers, we started getting more into Hip-Hop and making money from Hip-Hop, and being successful in Hip-Hop. He changed his name to Ol' Dirty Bastard. That was the name that I gave him. I ask for forgiveness for that as well as you can thank me for that. I say ask for forgiveness for that because sometimes a man doesn't make a name but the name makes the man.

And when I think back to Ason Unique, he was the kind of person that didn't have any beef. He kept himself super clean. He walked like Mr. Spock. He would challenge anybody in his cipher and every time he spoke, he spoke with wisdom. The radiance that he had, the beauty that he had, was just angelic.

And, as he became Ol' Dirty Bastard, he became more successful. He had a lot more money, a lot more fun, but yet he got further away from Ason Unique and this had happened to myself also. I was a person chasing life, instead of letting life flow through me.

But, what happened is that he had to look at himself. And when we can no longer be satisfied with ourselves and find happiness, which is total and complete satisfaction with yourself, you look for all kinds of things that will make you happy. And what does that turn into? Alcohol. Drugs. And sex, y'all. And the abuse of alcohol, drugs, and sex will take any one of us out of here.

I consider myself a wise man who knows right from wrong, but when I saw that he was doing wrong, I refrained from intervening or stepping in between because we got this thing in the hood, like, "He's a grown man. He can do what he wants." See, that's what's wrong with family. That's neglect. Don't neglect each other. Reach out. Help out.

Dirty told me and he told others his other cousins in his family, "Yo. I'm dying." Personally, and I'm going to be honest with you, I took it as, oh, he's just high. He's just talking out of his mouth. But it was real. He was talking from his heart.

We come from a big family. It's a blessing to come from a big family, but that also means that there's going to be a lot more sorrow. Each and every one of us has to face that day. Take righteousness into your heart. Take our love into our heart and apply it back to one another. So, don't take something that someone tells you from their mouth or from their heart as a joke. Everything is real. And if you don't believe that it's real, this can show you how real it can be. And we'll have another sorrowful moment.

I say peace and blessing to Ason Unique. I love you with all my heart. I love my famil,y and I strive to be the best I can and help anyone in my family. And I hope that you all will show that love to each other and help each other. Be one of those families that we will read about in the history books.

Peace and love

9

The Posthumous Mixed Tape

Outside of great musical prowess, drug abuse, and mad genius, Russell Tyrone Jones had one thing in common with greats like the extraordinary Jaco Pastorious, Miles Davis, Coltrane, Hendrix and other showbiz musical geniuses; he was a stage hog who would upstage anyone who tried to work with them.

When groups would invite ODB onto the stage when he was in the audience, he'd never humbly refuse. He never missed a chance to ham it up and overshadow whoever was performing. Narcissists with low self-esteem like ODB cannot help but feed off of the audience and push the envelope at another musician's expense.

A classic story of this happening involves a confrontation between Black Thought, the lead vocalist of the Philly-based group the Roots, who eventually had to almost go to blows with Dirt on stage. Dirt was hanging out at Irving Plaza, enjoying the show not long after his release from prison when Black Thought recognized him and called him up on stage.

The band graciously played "Shimmy Shimmy Ya" for him, but afterwards Dirt tried high-jacking the show.

Black Thought had enough and forced Dirt off stage. This pissed Dirt off and he retaliated. The two squared off. What ?uestlove doesn't mention, but some fans in the audience at Irving Plaza that Thursday night do, is that ODB was booed off the stage. It was said that Dirt hung his head and "shuffled" off the stage. The Roots' version contradicts the bloggers' and instead of shamefully shuffling off voluntarily, he was thrown off while being belligerent. The altercation was pulled off stage and broken up by handlers and bodyguards.

A similar incident happened when Dirt shared the stage with the Lost Boys. At the time Dirt was well into his career when Dante Ross received a call to see if Dirt was available to play a spur-of-the-moment show. Ross tells the story in his own words in his video blog series *Hip Hop History 101,* but the heart of the story follows:

For three thousand dollars, Dirt agreed to do the show. "Who am I doin' the show wit?" Dirt slurped into the phone.

"The Lost Boyz," Ross answered.

"Word. I'll meet you there." When Dirt got to the show, he brought a herd of about fifteen to twenty people. Management refused the entourage entry backstage and at that point "pandemonium," as Ross called it, broke out.

To alleviate the situation, management bent and allowed the entire crew into the venue. "But, the second your show's over," management said to Ross, "I'm throwing those animals the fuck outta here."

At the outset of the Lost Boys' set, Dirty gave his DAT to the soundman for his upcoming set. The Lost Boys were hitting their marks and the crowd was appreciative. At the end of their popular "Lifestyles of the Rich and Famous" song, the trio began working the crowd. Hyping the upcoming set, Mr. Cheeks started teasing the crowd, "D'you know who we have here for you tonight? You won't believe this shit! D'ya'll want me to tell who we have in the house tonight?"

The crowd answered with cheers of adulation.

"We have here with us tonight Ol' Dirty Bastard!" The crowd erupted into a burst of excitement and they were worked into a lather until Dirt finally came onto the stage, probably not what Mr. Cheeks expected or really wanted. After all, Dirt's set was coming up, and they had a couple of more songs left in the Lost Boyz's set.

Dirt grabbed the nearest mic, which was out of Mr. Cheeks' hand, and said, "Yo, you wanna see some Ol' Dirty Bastard? Aww, shit! You don't want none of this! I said, do you want to see some Ol' Muthafuckin' Dirty Bastard?"

The crowd hissed their approval, and they were feeding off of Dirt as much as he was feeding off of them.

"Yo, put that fuckin' DAT in," Dirt demanded. The soundman was shocked. He didn't know how to respond since he very well couldn't interrupt the Lost Boyz' show when Dirt was supposed to close out the night. He didn't fulfill Dirt's request. Dirt repeated, "Yo, drop that fuckin' DAT! Play my shit!"

The sound man just stupidly kept looking at Dirt not knowing what to do.

"Go head, nigga! Play my shit!" Dirt barked.

By this time, Dirt's people stormed the sound man's booth and forced him to put Dirt's music on. The crowd went berserk. Dirt launched into "Brooklyn Zoo", and he was enveloped in gracious applause. Dirt was lost in the moment, not caring about destroying the Lost Boyz's set. From this point on, it was the Ol' Dirty Bastard show. The Lost Boyz were devastated. Cheeks and Freaky Tah ascended on Ross, who was standing just offstage. They got in his face and said, "Yo, D, how can you let him do this to us?"

"Look, I had nothing to do with this," Ross said trying to save his ass. When Dirt's boys saw the Lost Boyz punking off Dirt's bread-and-butter man, they stepped to the Lost Boyz.

The entourage came in pushing and shoving, "Back the fuck up! Yo, back up!" There was scrambling and shouting slightly off stage while Dirt was going the fuck off doing "Give it to Ya Raw." He was in his glory. He was oblivious to what was going on until the pushing and shoving worked its way onto the stage. At that time the Lost Boyz just took their beef up with the real cause of all this, Dirt.

Dirt finished the show, and he and the Lost Boyz picked back up on the differences when Dirt came off stage. This time, though, when chests started bumping and the exaggerated posturing eclipsed the show, management and security swooped in and manhandled Dirt's people and the Lost Boyz's crew out onto the street.

"Dirty was on the outside calling me and couldn't get in," remembered Ross, who was allowed to stay.

◇◇◇

During his hay day with singles high on the charts, Dirt often got into confrontations at clubs. Sporting a commoner's attitude and mentality as a Rap superstar, there was always trouble to get into among "the people". Everyday-people don't always want to deal with a genius's eccentricities. The gifted, constantly in pursuit of acceptance and outside stimulation, are easily led astray by fans and friends.

People are always posting online their stories of meeting Dirt. For instance, one fan claims to have smoked dust with Dirt in a rave in 1999, a period where Dirt was an established "Ghetto Superstar," but there he was in the bathroom of a rave, smoking dust with a complete stranger. Supposedly, the story ends with Dirt going off and attacking people in the club. He was manhandled off of the premises. Whether or not this poster is lying is unclear, however, considering the pattern of behavior exhibited and the common threads to these stories, it is believable. Also, could everyone be lying?

Sometimes he would just go off and start wilin' out. Sometimes he would be half-eyes-open drunk or high on something, or both, and be a nuisance just because he was out of his head and talking crazy bullshit.

But sometimes, even in this state, when the lights came up and one of his favorite songs started thumpin', he could snap right into action and perform and kick major ass out of his head, pure drunken-master style.

◇◇◇

Once when he was on *Yo! MTV Raps*, he was able to pull off a classic Drunken Master performance. It was 1995.

In a bumper segment coming back from a commercial break, Ed Lover set up ODB to do a freestyle to lead into a video. Buddha Monk and some others were hanging around the set like cheap window dressings. Doctor Dre was at the turntable and he started up that single note that is hammered on "Shimmy Shimmy Ya."

Dirt had the hood up on his oversized, light gray hoodie, and he had a huge lumberjack red flannel shirt open like it was a jacket. The mic was pinned right on the middle of his chest. ODB was pacing in small circles on the set, not at all concerned with Ed Lover receiving the show and introducing him.

"My man Ol' Dirty Bastard is in the house!" Ed Lover said as Dirt bobbed around dancing in front of the turntable. With a wave of his hand, he tapped Dirt and got his attention. Ed made sure that he and Dirt were on their proper spot. "Right here. Still part of The Wu-Tang Clan. Ain't nothin' changed," Ed Lover said.

The camera closed in on Dirt and he began drunkenly slurring his words and talking through his teeth, his trademark style. It was no act. He licked his lips, and they began catching and reflecting the lights. "Drunkascanbe," he unintelligibly said, "I'm the drunken master style. Nobody can ever touch me. No one can ever feel me." The bass drums kicked in on the track and Dirt's vocals started in, "Oooh baby, I like it raaaw! Yeah baby, I like it raawww!" Dirt continued his rant, waving his arms, "Say that he loves me or she loves me," he babbled. "See, the blessings of this earth-"

"Dirty, Dirty," Ed Lover said, tapping him again to get his attention on the task at hand. "Hit me with some lyrics, man. Hit me with some lyrics."

Dirt cleared his throat and immediately launched into a freestyle right on beat, "Sometimes the lyrics," he dragged for emphasis the last syllable of "lyrics," "Just gotta come out. Make a laaayyddyy" he worked over the beat, "wanna scream and shout."

ODB went the fuck off. He started a rhyme, flip flopped it on itself, skipped beats, and cut it all up. Ed Lover and Dre were bobbing their heads in the background. Budda and the partner that he leaned his elbow on stood stock still, no expression or emotion on their faces. Then it was time for Dirt to stop. He missed the que. He was lost in the moment.

Dirt was sucking in breath like he was having some sort of spasm, slinging lines and abstract phrases on a whole different axis. "To the Holy Ghost catch what I'm dustin' ya'. To (or some garbled syllable keeping time with the beat) the neighborhood Ghostbusta." He was waving his arms and throwing his head from side to side like he was bobbing and weaving through a jungle full of vines and spider webs. His eyes were rolled, and he was taken over by the beat as if he really were entranced by the Holy Ghost.

He was in the zone and you could hear Ed Lover signaling in the background. It may have been a que. Dirt continued.

A point in the song came when it was the perfect time to stop. It was probably the planned time for Dirt to stop, but again, Dirt missed the que and continued. He used the dropped beat to spin off rhythm and fill the empty space, like Miles Davis would fill silence with whole, single notes and augmented half notes.

Dirt did another round, gyrating as if in a trance, "Always flex with the implex," he started hollering at the next level, "To the ladies bend to have sex," his voice squeaked on "sex" for he was screaming by this point. He sank into another line, but Ed stepped in to cut him short.

He laughed and grabbed Dirt. Dirt was still pushing the rhymes. Ed continued laughing and said, "Okay! No more! No more!" Dirt was pulled back to Earth. Ed Lover played it off. "He can go all night! He can rhyme all night! But we gotta go to my man's video." Dirt started pacing the set, covering his mouth, saying "Ah, ah, shh," as if even he was shocked by what just happened.

This was Dirt at his best. He shined. Everyone watching and all on the set knew that they had just witness something special. A rare, untamed, spontaneous moment of honest, raw talent exposing itself with unheralded purity.

It was also characteristic of how Dirt could steal a show and totally take the air out of the room, smothering anyone sharing the stage with him.

◇◇◇

Many acts in the '60s and '70s would say the same about playing after Jimi Hendrix. Arguments used to break out between promoters and managers because they didn't want to be on a bill with Jimi and have to follow him. If everything turned out right, he went on last to close the show and be a spectacle that no one had to try to outperform. ODB, like Jimi, was the closer. That is, of course, when he was on. It was tragic when he wasn't. But the fans understood.

The sad part of Dirt's unparalleled performance on *Yo! MTV Raps,* however, is the fact that, again, this was not an act. Dirt was blasted. He admittedly told those watching that he had forgotten what it was he wanted to do. Going off on a tangent and being lost in the moment, Dirt just went with the flow. He was using free association, digging deep into his unconscious for phrases and lines that would never be rationally or systematically thought up, created, or written down.

If he could've, perhaps, cultivated the drunken master act without being drunk, he would've had it made. Back in the day, Foster Brooks went from late night show to late night show with a drunken shtick. Watching old footage over the course of Brooks' career, a critical eye sees the discrepancies in authenticity between the performances with varying degrees of success in pulling it off and hitting his marks. But with Dirt, there was no doubt. From one drunken freestyle to the next, Dirt brought the goods organically from an inorganic inebriation.

◇◇◇

As a humorist, his lyrics and his delivery show how he was a comic genius as well. His blending of irreverent statements and, at times, an unrelenting meanness of Gansta Rap, was at the core of his style. Vocally, he used his tones and dramatic pronunciations to highlight ridiculous declarations. He used classic comedic devices along with a myriad of poetic devices. He used reversals, parody, self-deprecating humor, hyperbole, and traditional storytelling of the most bizarre scenarios.

One of his favorite modes of humor was his distorted cover songs. They were not quite parody and not quite tongue in cheek, but all the way off kilter. Dirt turned cover songs into his own brand of zaniness all while putting his heart and soul into it and putting forth the conviction of any great singer. No music critic can create a list of the Worst Cover Songs of all times without mentioning one of Dirt's covers.

Perhaps the favorite, worst cover is his collaboration with Macy Gray. They completely and unapologetically mutilate "Don't Go Breaking My Heart," made famous by Elton John and Kiki Dee. Other good, bad covers are Rick James's "Cold Blooded," the Foundations' "Why Do You Build Me Up," and Phil Collins' "Sussudio."

◇◇◇

When given the transitional periods of a Wu show, Dirt was known to have the most bugged-out monologues.

There is a Youtube video posted from a show at the Atrium in Atlanta. The Wu was opening up for Rage Against the Machine for The Wu Forever Triple Platinum Party. "Did you ever have your cocaine in your shoe and have the shit melt?" He asked when he had the stage and the rest of The Wu was hanging around between songs and taking swigs of beer.

His jumping topics would keep audiences laughing. "George Bush is an insane mothafucka. Don't fuck with that nigga; he's a gansta mothafucka," he was quoted as saying in one of these moments.

These types of non sequiturs, random and absurd thoughts, added a humorous element to an otherwise serious Wu live show.

There were times, however, when members of the group would become frustrated with Dirt. Sometimes members would just say, "Shut that nigga up!" Or they'd mockingly say, "That nigga's crazy."

There are times when frustration could be seen pronounced on RZA's face or other members of the group. On camera, Meth, RZA, and GZA each had to cover for him during interviews. When no one was around to save him from himself in an interview, like a well known MTV interview on 15/15 MTV News Special Edition with John Norris, his mouth and bizarre sense of humor were sure to get him into some type of trouble.

Other times, Wu members would be frustrated and angry at Dirt for hogging the show or derailing the show. Sometimes someone would just cut him off and send him to the back of the stage, but Dirt wasn't easily thwarted.

Once Dirt went off, he seldom knew when to stop and pull back, whether on stage, in an interview, or at a party. And that was his charm.

◇◇◇

Like Dirt's music, the stories and the memories of Ol' Dirty Bastard will live on. His story is a monument to anyone who cherishes individualism, artistic sincerity, and all out zaniness.

Looking back on his life may be a painful reminder of our vulnerabilities, our weaknesses, and our inability to truly connect with one another when we are at our lowest. Whether we try to reach out to help one another or not doesn't really matter anyway. When it comes down to it, ultimately, we are destined to fall short in intervening in someone's life because human existence is so singular, so solitary. Change comes from within the individual.

Dirt's mother didn't cry at his funeral. She said that when she saw him lying in his casket that he looked so peaceful, so at rest, that she knew he was no longer in pain. He was no longer being tortured by his inner demons. She cried for him all the time when he was alive. Why cry now?

Encore—The Hidden Bonus Track

The following is an open letter written by Dirt's Mom that was published on November 14, 2008.

Four years ago today marks one of the most tragic days in my life when I lost my son Rusty, whom many of you know as Ol' Dirty Bastard. For the past four years I have sat back and watched certain individuals try and tarnish my son's beliefs. My son loved every single one of his children and every single one of their mothers and provided for them all the best he could when he was alive. My son was an extremely generous soul. In the past four years, my daughter-in-law has portrayed me very poorly, Icelene. While I am very upset with my daughter-in-law's false remarks towards me, I am more upset by the way the other children Rusty had fathered and cherished are not being taken care of properly. I am also outraged that it appears Icelene has been diverting money away from the other children and taking out personal loans against Rusty's Estate Assets. She has gone through numerous attorneys and her new attorneys have racked up numerous amounts of legal fees and have accomplished nothing. The fans want my son's last album, which they are not allowing Koch to drop.

I'm not a lawyer or a judge, but the children's attorney, the Estate's lawyer Donald David and Jeremy Shure and the Judge Margarita Lopez Toress seem to have no interest in stopping Icelene from looting the estate. In fact many of the mothers have recently hired their own attorneys for the children, because some of them felt that the attorney that Judge Margarita Lopez Torres appointed for them wasn't properly representing their children. He hasn't showed up at depositions, he hasn't done anything to protect my grandchildren. How can you allow someone who has spent over six figures and taken out personal loans against estate assets to continue? Even the bonding company who bonds the Estate is fighting to get out because of the fraud she has committed on the Estate.

It also troubles me that Ferrar and Strauss, a division of Macmillan, are publishing a book about my son's life. After my son got out of prison, Dirty's manager, Jarred Weisfeld, and I received a call that

Rolling Stone wanted to do an interview with Dirty. We said okay and allowed the person to interview him. She came back for one more interview, which took place at a concert. The article never appeared in Rolling Stone, however it did appear in The Village Voice. After my son passed, this author who knew my son for only a few hours decided to write a book and asked Jarred and myself to take part in it. We declined and asked that she not use any part of the interview she conducted with my son, in her book, but she did. I am asking all of Dirty's fans to boycott this book as none of the proceeds are going to his children and this author's motives and intentions seem to be to disgrace my son's legacy.

Also, quotes from lawyer Robert Shapiro, in yesterday's newspaper, are shameful. The fact that an attorney who represented my son for less than a minute would comment and speculate on my son's health to get his name in print is disgraceful. The world knows that Robert Shapiro was not really my son's attorney and his real attorney was like a second father to him and his name is Peter Frankel, one of the only people who went above and beyond the call of duty for my son and whom I love dearly for that.

I hope next year, my son's final album will be released for the 5th Anniversary of his passing. It pains me to have to write this on the day of his passing, but I needed to address this.

I know my son would have been at that rally in Chicago when the first African American President was elected and I'm sure he would have gone up on stage and grabbed the microphone as only he could.

Lastly today is a very sad day not only for me, but also for my entire family including Dirty's father and his siblings and children. I will always love my son, Rusty, and I will always make sure all of his children are taken care of.

His loving mother, Cherry Jones

Author's Bio:

Spencer Sadler is a freelance writer from Indiana, PA, a Pittsburgh suburb. An educator by trade, Sadler writes for magazines, newspapers, and online sites. In his spare time, he loves surfing the net for headlines and blogging on politics. He's also a sports nut who supports his hometown teams.

ORDER FORM

WWW.AMBERBOOKS.COM

Fax Orders: 480-283-0991
Telephone Orders: 602-743-7211
Postal Orders: Send Checks & Money Orders to:
    Amber Books
    1334 E. Chandler Blvd., Suite 5-D67, Phoenix, AZ 85048

Online Orders: E-mail: Amberbk@aol.com

____*God Made Dirt: The Life & Times of Ol' Dirty Bastard,* ISBN _____, $16.95
____*Black Eyed Peas: Unauthorized Biography,* ISBN 978-0-9790976-4-5, $16.95
____*Red Hot Chili Peppers: In the Studio,* ISBN #: 978-0-9790976-5-2, $16.95
____*Dr. Dre In the Studio,* ISBN#: 0-9767735-5-4, $16.95
____*Kanye West in the Studio,* ISBN #: 0-9767735-6-2, $16.95
____*Tupac Shakur—(2Pac) In The Studio,* ISBN#: 0-9767735-0-3, $16.95
____*Jay-Z...and the Roc-A-Fella Dynasty,* ISBN#: 0-9749779-1-8, $16.95
____*Your Body's Calling Me: The Life & Times of "Robert" R. Kelly,* ISBN#: 0-9727519-5-52, $16.95
____*Ready to Die: Notorious B.I.G.,* ISBN#: 0-9749779-3-4, $16.95
____*Suge Knight: The Rise, Fall, and Rise of Death Row Records,* ISBN#: 0-9702224-7-5, $21.95
____*50 Cent: No Holds Barred,* ISBN#: 0-9767735-2-X, $16.95
____*Aaliyah—An R&B Princess in Words and Pictures ,* ISBN#: 0-9702224-3-2, $10.95
____*You Forgot About Dre: Dr. Dre & Eminem,* ISBN#: 0-9702224-9-1, $10.95
____*Divas of the New Millenium,* ISBN#: 0-9749779-6-9, $16.95
____*Michael Jackson: The King of Pop,* ISBN#: 0-9749779-0-X, $29.95

Name:_____

Company Name:_____

Address:_____

City:_____State: _____Zip:_____

Telephone: (____)_____E-mail: _____

For Bulk Rates Call: 602-743-7211　　　　　**ORDER NOW**

God Made Dirt	$16.95	☐ Check ☐ Money Order ☐ Cashiers Check
Black Eyed Peas	$16.95	☐ Credit Card: ☐ MC ☐ Visa ☐ Amex ☐ Discover
Red Hot Chili Peppers	$16.95	
Dr. Dre In the Studio	$16.95	CC#_____
Kanye West	$16.95	Expiration Date:_____
Tupac Shakur	$16.95	
Jay-Z...	$16.95	**Payable to:**
Your Body's Calling Me:	$16.95	Amber Books
Ready to Die: Notorious B.I.G.,	$16.95	1334 E. Chandler Blvd., Suite 5-D67
Suge Knight:	$21.95	Phoenix, AZ 85048
50 Cent: No Holds Barred,	$16.95	**Shipping:** $5.00 per book. Allow 7 days for delivery.
Aaliyah—An R&B Princess	$10.95	**Sales Tax:** Add 7.05% to books shipped to Arizona
Dr. Dre & Eminem	$10.95	addresses.
Divas of the New Millenium,	$16.95	
Michael Jackson: The King of Pop	$29.95	**Total enclosed:** $_____

www.ingramcontent.com/pod-product-compliance
Lightning Source LLC
Chambersburg PA
CBHW051722090426
42738CB00010B/2044